HAUNTED
MIAMI VALLEY

HAUNTED MIAMI VALLEY

JENNIFER EBLIN

Published by Haunted America
A Division of The History Press
Charleston, SC 29403
www.historypress.net

Copyright © 2010 by Jennifer Eblin
All rights reserved

First published 2010

Manufactured in the United States

ISBN 978.1.60949.022.5

Library of Congress CIP data applied for.

Notice: The information in this book is true and complete to the best of our knowledge. It is offered without guarantee on the part of the author or The History Press. The author and The History Press disclaim all liability in connection with the use of this book.

All rights reserved. No part of this book may be reproduced or transmitted in any form whatsoever without prior written permission from the publisher except in the case of brief quotations embodied in critical articles and reviews.

CONTENTS

Acknowledgements 7
Introduction 9

1. Miami County 11
2. Montgomery County 16
3. Champaign County 44
4. Butler County 49
5. Warren County 62
6. Darke County 80
7. Shelby County 83
8. Clark County 88
9. Greene County 93
10. Preble County 104

Works Cited 109
About the Author 111

ACKNOWLEDGEMENTS

I'd like to thank a number of people involved with making this book a reality. First and foremost are the girls and guys I spent time with in high school. If not for them spending hours driving around aimlessly with me and checking out haunted sites, I doubt I'd still find the topic interesting today. I'd also like to thank the writers and owners of Headstoners, who graciously let me use photographs of Hell House.

A special thanks also goes out to my boyfriend, Brian, who spent many months listening to me ramble about haunted places and talk to myself. He also kept me on track and visited many sites with me, even taking some photos himself. All of my friends deserve a special thanks, especially Blake and Katy for having faith in the book and, of course, my parents.

A special man also deserves a nod here: Dennis Gray. Though he's no longer with us, he always had faith in my writing and encouraged me to keep writing. Special thanks also go out to The History Press and Joseph Gartrell. Thanks for taking a chance on a local girl who loves haunted sites and had literally no experience writing more than a few hundred words on the topic!

INTRODUCTION

Few states have a specific region with its own nickname, but Ohio does. The Miami Valley region covers a good portion of the southwest area of the state, in addition to parts of central Ohio. It's the area around the Great Miami Valley and even includes a few suburbs of Cincinnati, such as Hamilton and Middletown.

The Miami Valley has large cities, small towns, even villages, and of course, it also has ghosts, haunted sites and legends. These ghost stories tell the history of Ohio, from the early days when Native Americans called the land home to more modern times. Stories cover major manufacturing plants in the state, rural communities with more cows than people and large cities.

The tales are sometimes humorous and oftentimes dark. You'll hear about poor young women who couldn't handle the difficulties life threw at them and a woman who was brutally murdered with a fireplace log. You'll hear stories of scary creatures that stalk the Miami Valley, including a serpent creature and a Bigfoot-style creature.

It's a place many are proud to call home, myself included. This is the area where I went on my first ghost hunt, the place where I camped out late at night, in the middle of cemeteries and buildings, hoping for a glimpse of a ghost. As a teenager, I visited a few of the sites mentioned in this book frequently, sometimes on a weekly basis. Though I have had some weird experiences, I have yet to see a real ghost—but I'm not giving up hope just yet.

I have had my fair share of unique experiences in the area, including the house I grew up in and the house where my parents still live. I remember

Introduction

little things happening when I was a child: the modem kept unplugging itself from the wall for no reason and the house made odd noises. We were always told that it was just the sounds of an old house settling. For a house not even forty years old at the time, it sure settled a lot!

One night, a few friends and I became brave enough to hold a mock séance in the house, using an addition made to the original house. After waiting for everyone to leave the house, we formed a circle and started "talking" to the spirits. We asked for someone to knock three times on the garage wall if anyone was there. To this day, we can't explain why we clearly heard three knocks on that exact wall.

When my boyfriend and I moved into our new-old house in Franklin, I felt a little odd. We put it off to moving into a new house after living in an apartment for nearly two years. The house dates back to the late nineteenth or early twentieth century and, at some point, was divided into a duplex, with additions added to the back of both sides.

As we were on a tight timeframe and needed to move into the new house in less than a week, I ended up carting down a carload late at night. After carrying everything inside, I sat down for a minute, just to catch my breath. Imagine my surprise when I clearly heard the sounds of something moving upstairs. Maybe it was an echo caused by our neighbors walking around in the middle of the night, or maybe we were sharing the house with some people not paying their share of the rent.

My stories aren't the only ones in the area, and there are certainly other interesting tales to be told. These stories belong to the region, and many have their roots in the history of the area. The Miami Valley has a long history, but unfortunately, some of the historic structures across the region no longer exist today. They were torn down to make room for new schools, demolished for highways and torn down and rebuilt. If you visit any of the sites mentioned here, be respectful of your surroundings.

Cemeteries in the area are already closing and locking their gates at night to stop trespassing and vandalism. Vandals have destroyed or damaged a number of important items, including the Johnny Morehouse tombstone at Woodland Cemetery. Ruining something or leaving your mark does little except help cut off access for those who come after.

When you're ready for a haunted tour in the Miami Valley, start with Miami County. Home to Piqua, Troy and my hometown of Tipp City, it's a place full of history and haunted sites.

CHAPTER 1
MIAMI COUNTY

One of the largest cities in Miami County is Piqua. Originally known as Fort Pickawillany, this small settlement first appeared in 1747. By 1780, the area was home to two separate towns: Upper Piqua and Lower Piqua. At the turn of the century, the two towns merged and formed Piqua. The city is also known for the small town of Rossville, which became part of Piqua. This settlement began in 1833 and was made of freed slaves.

The Fort Piqua Hotel, which is also known as Hotel Fort Piqua and the Piqua Hotel, has a long and involved history. William P. Orr and Samuel K. Statler are responsible for the building itself, which was built between 1890 and 1891 and was originally known as the Plaza. Sitting at the corner of Main and High Streets, the two busiest streets in town, the building immediately attracted customers. Stanhope Boal, who owned the Favorite Stove and Range Company, purchased the building, renovated the interior and changed the name to the Favorite Hotel in 1914.

Throughout the history of the hotel, several presidents spent the night. William Howard Taft, Warren G. Harding and even Teddy Roosevelt laid their heads here. During the swinging 1920s, the hotel had its own bookie and illegal betting parlor. Following Prohibition, Piqua received its first bar, thanks to the hotel. As early as the 1940s, the hotel prohibited desegregation, letting African American patrons sit side by side with Caucasian customers.

The building, with over seventy thousand square feet, began falling into a state of disarray during the 1970s. At one point it served as a bus depot and a transient hotel before closing its doors completely. Locals cited the

The old Fort Piqua Hotel as it looks today. *Courtesy of the City of Piqua.*

building as an example of urban decay in smaller cities. Developers frequently created plans to turn the space into something else, but the high cost of the renovation work turned off many.

Finally, the City of Piqua decided to take matters into its own hands. In 2001, the city created its own nonprofit organization and set about raising the funds needed for the restoration work. It took over two years and $20 million, but eventually it reopened, under the name Fort Piqua Plaza. It once again provided a necessary space for residents of Piqua. Restorers preserved the original chandelier, staircase and stained-glass windows.

Despite its history, the Piqua Hotel also had problems that some believe led to the hauntings. While some of the stories are true, others are merely the work of overactive imaginations and creative minds. When the hotel was building its sewer system, one of the trench diggers was accidentally buried alive.

Another story claims that a worker was nearly burned to death after he accidentally fell into a barrel of acid. Stories also claim that workers digging the basement stumbled upon a bunch of skeletons and that a man committed suicide by hanging in a hotel room. There's also a story about a luggage cart that accidentally flipped over and crushed a porter. According to a different version of the story, the porter was accidentally crushed to death in the elevator.

The one story that's actually true involves a criminal and a police officer. During the 1970s, the two men shot and killed each other in the hotel's lobby. Supposedly the criminal was trying to escape custody when the event occurred and the shots were fired in front of an old mirror. Legend says that the mirror remained in the building for years and may even still be there.

Those stories, however, don't explain the ghosts living in the hotel. The ghost of a former waiter wanders the building, and former owner Stanhope Boal's spirit never left one of the rooms. Previous occupants and renters of the space claim to have experienced odd things, including hearing weird noises and seeing shadows on the walls.

Miami County

Piqua is also home to a haunted building called the Old Stone Front Home. Legend says that a woman who lived in the building died. On the night before her funeral, her young son disappeared, and many people thought the boy was taken. They didn't think he would abandon his mother and searched for him for days before giving up. Twenty years after his disappearance, a group of workers cleaned out a well and found his body. The little boy is sometimes seen and heard crying in the building.

Not far away from Piqua is Miami County's Troy, Ohio. Originally named a city in 1808, its location on the Miami and Erie Canal and close proximity to several roads led to the city being named the county seat. By 1846, the city was home to churches, a plow factory, sawmills, flour mills, warehouses, newspapers and shops. The town only continued to grow over the years when the Hobart Corporation and Hobart Brothers Corporation settled in town.

Troy has its own crybaby bridge, a popular legend that exists in dozens of smaller towns across the Midwest. Most stories center on a poor or young mother who tosses or accidentally drops her baby over the bridge. Troy's crybaby bridge sits on LeFevre Road and Lost Creek. Local legend claims that in the 1940s or 1950s, a couple crossing the bridge got into an accident. The baby flew from the car and landed in the creek. The couple survived, but no sign was ever found of the child. Those visiting the bridge late at night sometimes claim to hear his mournful cries.

Troy also has the haunted Polecat Road, which has multiple stories told about it. The most popular involves a motorcycle rider who crashed and died on the road years ago. Just down the street is a spot some claim the Ku Klux Klan once used to lynch people. This led to stories that the man was killed by the KKK or died trying to escape their hands. His ghost typically takes the form of a green light that seems to float down the road.

Also in Troy is the haunted Grove Cemetery. This small cemetery dates back to the nineteenth century and is fairly difficult to find because it's hidden by trees and has only a small gravel road. Local legend claims that in the 1870s, a young woman stopped by the cemetery to visit her father's or grandfather's grave. A man rushed out of the shadows, grabbed her and killed her after raping her. Some claim to hear a woman's screams coming from the exact spot where the incident occurred. Other stories are told about ghostly footsteps walking through the cemetery.

The Bradford Sanitarium turns up on frequent lists of haunted sites, though the building itself no longer exists. The town dates back to 1865, when the city limits laid within nearby Darke County. The town built up around railroad workers who lived in the area. Today, portions of the town remain in Darke County, while others reside in Miami County.

The sanitarium originally opened in the 1920s. While it was once home to dozens of people, the building caught fire and burned in 1935. The poor and mentally ill were brought to the building, where they suffered through early psychological treatments designed to "cure" them. Visitors who dared to enter the property after dark reported seeing ghostly orbs floating through the sky.

The haunted Horseshoe Bend Road is located in West Milton. This small village dates back to at least 1807, when plots of land were sold. Originally named for poet John Milton, the village changed its name in 1817, as another town was known as Milton. In 1834, West Milton officially became incorporated. Legend says that a group of kids was playing in the woods and decided to split up for hide-and-seek. Only one boy was left, and the kids eventually found him dead, hanging from a tree. His ghost is sometimes seen near the water under the bridge on Horseshoe Bend Road.

One of the more popular spots is Staley Road in New Carlisle. The road is partially in Miami County and partially in Clark County and has multiple stories told about it. The Forgotten Ohio website offers a story passed on by a reader. A group of young people was driving down the road when they saw someone lying down in the middle of the road. They turned around, and no one was there. Everyone in the car clearly saw the man there when they passed by originally.

Staley Road is popular with local teens, in part because the road has such a dark and spooky feel. The trees seem to curve over the road, blocking out light even on the brightest days. Generations of students at nearby Bethel High School have passed around stories, and even the parents like to get involved. For some, it's simply a matter of keeping the kids away from the road, which curves and looks fairly dangerous. One of the former residents of the town reports an experience she had:

> One night my friends and I decided to drive around Staley Road, just checking things out. There was a large group of us, so we decided to take

Miami County

Staley Road looks dark and ominous, even during the daylight hours. *Author's collection.*

two separate cars. After we got out there, we stopped the car and started looking around. We noticed that the other car was missing and couldn't find them anywhere, so we turned around and went back to our friend's house. They were sitting in the driveway with the lights off and their emergency flashers turned on. They were on their way down the road when the electrical system went crazy: the radio started switching channels, the lights went off and the flashers came on. They tried everything and couldn't get it to work. Even our friend's dad couldn't fix things. After trying for a few minutes, it just stopped and went back to working normal. I've been down that road on my own a few times and I always get this creepy feeling, like someone is watching me in the woods.

According to some locals who lived in the area previously, satanic cults practiced in the woods on Staley Road during the 1970s. Neighbors began finding mutilated bodies of animals in the woods and sometimes saw dark figures in robes walking through the woods. Rumors also exist that a dead body was found in the woods during the 1970s. Stories of voices talking in the woods and guns being shot are also told. In addition, a large number of people report having electrical problems with their cars on this stretch of road.

CHAPTER 2
MONTGOMERY COUNTY

Montgomery County is perhaps best known for its capital city of Dayton, but it's also home to a few well-known ghosts. As one of the largest and most populated areas in the Miami Valley, it's not surprising that it deserves such a long chapter.

The suburb of Centerville is home to several ghosts. Originally, the town was known as Centreville, after the hometown in New Jersey or citizen Benjamin Robbins. Locals preferred the name because it was centered in between two other towns and two rivers. The United States Post Office changed the spelling of the town name to Centerville in 1900.

In the early days, locals replaced log cabins and log buildings with buildings made from local limestone. About thirty of those original stone buildings still exist in the town, and they are on the National Register of Historic Places. In 1968, Centerville was officially named a city.

Locals claim that the Centerville Cemetery is haunted. According to legend, the man buried at the Wolfe Mausoleum kept two wolves as pets during his life. When he died, he asked that the wolves be buried with him. When you walk past the mausoleum, you may hear the ghostly howls of the two wolves.

Centerville is also home to the haunted Town Hall Theatre. The building dates back to 1908, when it was actually used as the town hall. Over the decades, the building played host to graduation ceremonies, council meetings and other events. The town government continued to use the building until

1985. A few years later, plans were begun to turn the town hall building into a performing arts building or theatre. A full renovation of the building started in 1992, and the theatre now puts on a number of performances every year.

No one knows exactly where the ghost of the theatre came from, but they do know that he has definite opinions about what happens on stage. He occasionally acts out, especially if he doesn't like the play. He isn't fond of any play that features references to sex, nudity or cursing. Those who worked there claim he turns off the pilot light.

The lights surrounding the stage frequently flicker, and stories are also told about the basement area. It's said that the basement remains dark even when lights are on, and visitors always feel cold. A tall man with a dark beard, resembling Abraham Lincoln, is sometimes seen peering from a window on one of the upper floors.

Another haunted spot in Centerville is a house located on Social Road Row. Elizabeth Bradford moved into the house in 1838 with her husband and lived there until 1844. The owners believe she's the ghost haunting their home. A former couple who lived in the house heard the sounds of glass and china breaking one night. The next morning, they discovered that nothing was missing or broken.

Located over the Mad River in Dayton is a modern-day version of the crybaby bridge. The story says that a teenage girl got pregnant and decided to keep the baby. Though her boyfriend urged her to end the pregnancy, she followed through, thinking that he'd eventually change his mind. Somehow, she managed to keep the entire pregnancy a secret from her parents. After the baby was born, she tossed it over the side of the bridge. The story says that those traveling over the bridge after dark can hear the sounds of the baby crying.

Miamisburg has a long history and several ghosts. Zachariah Hole arrived in the area at the end of the eighteenth century and referred to the town as Hole's Station. Originally, he and his family were the only residents, but this quickly changed as settlers arrived from Pennsylvania. They eventually changed the name to Miamisburg to honor the Miami Indians living in the area.

In 1818, four Pennsylvania residents purchased ninety lots at public auction. These plots were part of a town referred to as Miamisburg. Fourteen years later, the area had enough residents to become a village. It would take nearly one hundred years for the neighborhood to officially become a city in the state of Ohio.

The cemetery at Library Park dates back to 1850. At the time, Miamisburg was in desperate need of a new cemetery, as the first cemetery was getting full. The town council eventually picked a location on the east side of Miamisburg, the exact spot where Library Park now sits. The bodies from the original cemetery were moved to this spot, and the city erected a fence around the property. In 1864, the town founded the Hill Grove Cemetery and once again moved the bodies.

This would have been the end of the cemetery's story, if not for an event in 1965. By then, the area was set aside for a city park. The plans called for a large fountain in the center of the park, which required new water lines. City workers laying the water lines stumbled across an old-fashioned coffin made of cast iron. Inside was the body of a man. The city eventually moved this body to the Highland Cemetery.

The area underwent a number of changes over the years. The city added a bandstand and the aforementioned water fountain, creating a public park. In 1909, work began on a Carnegie Library, which was completed the following year. A memorial was added to commemorate local men who died in World War I, and other stones followed for the Korean Conflict and the Vietnam Conflict. In 1981, the Dayton Montgomery County Public Library opened a branch in this location.

The former cemetery at Library Park has an interesting ghost story. In 1884, a young woman was murdered on the spot. Her ghost kept returning to the spot for a number of days, and the story even appeared in local newspapers. According to a newspaper article, the figure started appearing every night at 9:00 p.m. Locals recognized the girl as a girl who was previously murdered.

The ghost walked through the park with her head down, and the paper reported that she seemed in "deep thought." At one point, one thousand people turned up at the cemetery, all hoping to catch a glimpse of the ghost. The article goes on to state that people attacked the figure with guns and knives. Citizens began removing bodies from the cemetery in the hopes of getting rid of the ghost. Eventually, all bodies were moved to Hill Grove Cemetery. Yet there are still stories of the young girl wandering the area, still wearing the same white dress she wore when she first made her appearance.

Montgomery County

The Arby's in Miamisburg is haunted by several ghosts, oddly enough. This modern-day fast-food restaurant sits on a busy intersection, and none of the adjoining buildings reports any ghostly activity. One of the ghosts is that of a man with a bald head. During the early morning or late at night, the man appears, sitting next to the oven. Employees report feeling someone watching them or even pulling on their clothes and hair. There are also stories told about employees hearing kids laughing long after the dining room is closed.

Also in Miamisburg is the older Hill Grove Cemetery. This is where the bodies from the old Library Park cemetery were moved. With some of the oldest graves dating back to the 1800s, it's not surprising that it has multiple ghosts. One is that of a local girl who was raised in a religious family. She and her preacher father argued frequently over religion, and when she refused to believe, he disowned her. After her death, the family had a Bible tombstone installed on her grave. The Bible sometimes appears broken, as if she still maintains her earthly beliefs.

The other ghost is that of another young girl and is similar to the story told about Woodland Cemetery. Visitors to the cemetery sometimes see a young girl sitting on the grave of her mother. When they ask if she needs help, she disappears. Some have seen her and heard her crying, only to turn around seconds later and find her gone.

Fudge Road traipses across several counties, including Montgomery County. This stretch of road has two separate crybaby bridges, one of which is close to Miamisburg. The story says that on a cool April night in 1981, an abused wife finally decided to escape from her husband. She grabbed her four-day-old baby and ran off. Her husband caught her just as she reached the bridge. She begged for her life and the life of their child, but to no avail. All he wanted was for her to come back, and to entice her, he dangled their child over the side of the bridge. As the two continued fighting, the child slowly died. The man tossed the child into the water and ran into a nearby cornfield, dragging his wife behind him.

The woman's mother eventually became worried when she heard no word from her daughter. She knew that the woman needed help caring for the new baby and tried calling and stopping by. She finally called the police, who investigated but couldn't find them. A few weeks later, the man's body was found dead in the fields, apparently of starvation. No trace of the mother or the baby was ever found, but some believe they still haunt the old bridge.

The Dayton suburb of Trotwood is home to Hara Arena and a haunted house. The Rattigan family owned the house and rented it to the Jaycees for use as a haunted house during the Halloween season. The Jaycees continually used the house in the 1980s until it burned down. A former resident of the house was murdered by an unknown assailant. The murderer heard rumors that the owner kept large amounts of cash in his house. He broke into the house and decapitated the man with an axe.

Legend says that the man did keep money around the house and that he watches over the building to keep his money safe. Workers had problems with lights coming on and off, heard footsteps when the house was empty and saw items moving on their own. Frequent cold spots were experienced in the house, and workers felt uncomfortable even when others were around.

Dawnview Avenue is located on the east side of Dayton and is the site of a haunted house. The presence in the house is so strong that it's difficult to find anyone willing to live in the house, at least for very long. Even when it became a HUD house, residents tended to leave in a year or less. A former resident believes it's because of the violent spirit that stays there. The resident claimed the ghost attacked her and created the smell of urine, which spread throughout the house.

The inpatient unit at Hospice of Dayton is also rumored to be haunted. Workers refer to the ghosts as the kids because they frequently see the ghosts of small children roaming through the hallways.

Another suburb of Dayton is the town of Oakwood. Oakwood was a haven for farmers and was mainly known for the farms in the area, up until the Great Dayton Flood occurred. Following this event in 1913, newspapers advertised to Dayton residents, pointing out that Oakwood was higher than Dayton. The town became incorporated in 1908 and became known as one of the more affluent neighborhoods in the Miami Valley. Orville Wright and John Patterson both owned homes in the area that still remain today.

The Oakwood High School is haunted by two ghosts. The school dates back to the 1920s, but before the school was built, a private home stood

Oakwood High School is much larger than the photo indicates and hides several ghosts. *Author's collection.*

there. A young girl who haunts the junior hallway is believed to be connected to the former home. Many students and workers have seen the girl sitting on a bench at night.

The other ghost is that of a former student who killed himself at the school. Students claim that he hanged himself there either in the 1960s or the 1970s. He's the ghost behind the odd footsteps heard through the school. Some students have also seen him from the corner of their eye, but when they turn, he's gone.

The Amber Rose Restaurant is one of the most famous haunted spots in Dayton. Located on Valley Street, the restaurant is haunted by a former owner's daughter. Owners call the ghost Chickee and claim she manifests by playing music and sometimes breaking dishes.

The Bessie Little Bridge is (not surprisingly) haunted by a woman named Bessie Little. The event that occurred here is tragic and sad. A heat wave struck Dayton in 1896, and citizens did everything possible to escape the heat. E.L. Harper Jr. was in town from Cincinnati visiting family when he decided to climb into the nearby water.

Not long after climbing into the water, he spotted what he thought was a shoe floating in the water. When he got closer, he realized it was actually a shoe attached to a woman's leg. He ran to a nearby boathouse owned by Charles L. Phillips and asked for help. The men phoned the police and dragged the foot from the water. Originally, authorities found no evidence of foul play. The truth, which they later uncovered, was shocking.

Police eventually uncovered the rest of the body of the woman in the water and identified her as Bessie Little. When her mother learned of her death, she appeared surprised, but not overly so. She told authorities that her adopted daughter and husband had been fighting frequently because of her bad behavior, and he eventually told her to leave. Her mother told authorities that someone came back for her clothing and personal items, but she hadn't seen her daughter in weeks.

Eventually, her mother confessed that Bessie was pregnant. She told police that she assumed her daughter killed herself because of the disgrace she made of her family. It's hard to imagine this happening today, but at the time, an unmarried woman becoming pregnant was a scandal, made even worse if the father of the child refused to marry her, as happened in Bessie's case. The case was made even more shocking when her mother told police to bury Bessie in Potter's Field. She had disgraced the family, and as far as they were concerned, she was no longer part of the family.

The police eventually brought in Albert Frantz for questioning. He told the police that he knew Bessie was missing because he had tried seeing her at her boardinghouse. He believed that she went back to her family and he didn't ask them, because they didn't approve of their relationship. He also stated that she was carrying his child and had told him about it months before but claimed to have no knowledge of her death.

What Albert didn't know was that Judge Kreitzer had already contacted the police. He stated that Frantz visited his office, told him of the body in the water and asked for advice on what to do, as he either killed her or knew how she died. Witnesses in the case began coming forward, allowing police to trace her last days.

A woman by the name of Ella Bell identified Bessie based on her clothing. The two women met while living at the Cooper Hotel, where Frantz footed the bill for Bessie's room. Her dentist later identified the body based on a gold filling he had placed in her mouth. Her landlord, Minnie Freese, provided the most damning evidence. Had things happened differently, police may have closed the case.

Freese told authorities that Bessie moved into her boardinghouse on August 20, when Frantz paid her bill. She lived there until August 28, and Freese remembered seeing Frantz frequently visiting her there. However, Freese also told authorities that she had a talk with Bessie, during which the young girl told her she had done something bad and was thinking of putting an end to it. This led even more credence to the suicide theory.

At the official inquiry into her death, Judge Kreitzer came to testify but said very little. He told authorities that he couldn't violate client confidentiality but did admit that he talked to someone about her death on August 29, the day after she went missing. Three teenage boys later came forward, claiming that they found blood and a broken hairclip on the bridge, indicating some kind of a struggle. The combs were identified as belonging to Bessie.

The police immediately dug up Bessie's body, and it was examined again by a medical expert. This investigation revealed two clear bullet holes on the right side of her head. Her former landlord revealed to police that she suspected Frantz, telling them that Bessie had a date planned with him on the night she disappeared. After a quick dinner, the young woman had started off across Fifth Street, planning to meet him for a buggy ride. Freese also stated that Frantz came the next day to pay Bessie's rent and told her that the two had never met up the night before.

The Ridge Street Bridge, as it was known at the time, became a sightseeing spot for locals and tourists alike. Over one thousand people turned up on the day the case was announced, all trying to look into the water and take home souvenirs. Police eventually had to block off the bridge completely just to finish their investigation.

It didn't take long for new evidence and new witnesses to arrive. A couple from Vandalia reported hearing a woman scream and a gunshot around 7:30 p.m. on the bridge on the night of Bessie's disappearance, and a second couple living in the area also heard the gunshots. As the witnesses came forward, Frantz was placed in police custody, and the local newspapers ran constant stories about the murder.

Eventually, authorities decided to try Frantz with Bessie's murder. Frantz pled not guilty, giving police a fantastical version of what happened that fateful night. He claimed that they did take a buggy ride but Bessie killed herself. When they reached the bridge, she cried out, grabbed his gun and shot herself twice. Panicked, he threw her in the water because he worried that he'd be blamed for her death.

His version of events was almost immediately discredited. The medical examiner used Bessie's actual skull and showed that the first shot killed her instantly. She never could have shot herself twice. Her mother testified that she never objected to their relationship and that the two had courted for almost a year. After seeing Albert sneaking around her barn and trying to sneak into their home, she had forbidden him from coming back or seeing Bessie. That was when Bessie left.

A local pastor testified that Frantz told him on the night of her murder that Bessie had killed herself. Frantz also told the pastor that he couldn't go to the police because he didn't want his father to know what happened. He told his brother what happened. It later came out that his brother and the pastor were the two who visited the judge.

For all the evidence indicting Frantz, there was just as much in support of his theory. A former friend testified that Bessie had threatened suicide before. Her landlady once again came forward, this time saying that she saw Frantz crying after Bessie turned down his proposal and often saw Bessie fighting with him. A doctor even came forward saying that he believed it was possible she shot herself twice.

Attorneys presented their own version of events. They claimed that Little and Frantz were dating and she left home to be with him. He paid all her bills until she confessed that she was pregnant. The two met for a buggy ride, and Frantz went into a rage, shooting her twice and leaving her body on the bridge. He then decided to throw her over the side, believing police would think it was suicide.

It took only two hours for the jury to return with a guilty verdict. Both he and his brother were practically carried from the courtroom, while his father openly cried. The jury called for the death penalty, and it was scheduled for May 13, 1897. Though his attorneys were denied a new trial, his appeals did postpone the death sentence. Albert even wrote to the governor, still maintaining his innocence.

Frantz was strapped into the electric chair at the Ohio State Penitentiary and the sentence was carried out on November 19, 1897, after his last appeal was denied. His family had his body buried in New Carlisle's Studebaker

Montgomery County

Cemetery. The following month, the Little family moved Bessie's remains to Woodland Cemetery, but Bessie's ghost still haunts the bridge. The bridge itself was replaced, but Bessie and her legacy still remain.

The Dayton Country Club has hosted some amazing parties over its history, and some of those parties never seem to end. Those working after hours, and even the owners, have heard the sounds of people laughing and music playing, as if a party is going on. Of course, when they attempt to investigate, they find no evidence of people or a party.

The Dayton Masonic Temple, now known as the Dayton Masonic Center, is another famously haunted site in the city. Situated on the river and found on the National Register of Historic Places, it's one of the most famous buildings in Dayton. The building dates back to the mid-1920s, but its most popular ghost only dates to 1962.

Legend claims that George was once a Mason and now haunts the building. Some visitors have also heard the sounds of a pair of women's high heel shoes walking through the building. Stories are also told about a possible ghost haunting the balcony outside the third-floor Commandery Asylum and another ghost on the first floor. Legend says a former member died in this area.

The website Forgotten Ohio lists a story told by a member of the Masons. The member claims that the elevators malfunction often, sometimes moving between two levels. She's experienced the sound of the woman walking and noticed the water fountains coming on. She also had an unusual experience involving seeing a woman walking through the women's restroom, only to find herself alone in the room.

Dayton's Masonic Temple remains practically unchanged on its exterior. *Courtesy of user Nyttend, via Wikimedia Commons.*

When the city built a hospital in 1867, it's doubtful that the same building would be at the center of ghost stories centuries later, but that's exactly what happened with the Dayton VA Medical Center. Originally, the hospital helped those returning from the Civil War, and it seems as though some of those people aren't ready to leave.

General Marsena Patrick stayed in Freedom House, one of the buildings on the campus, and it's also where he took his last breaths after a severe battle with epilepsy. He now manifests his spirit in the form of a gray mist. Visitors to Freedom House also sometimes hear the sounds of a party dating back to the 1870s. Liberty House at the hospital is also haunted. Officials have experienced problems with audio and video equipment inside the building.

St. Elizabeth's Medical Center saved the lives of thousands of patients over the years and birthed as many babies but also saw as many deaths. The hospital opened in 1878, run by the Franciscan Sisters. Its location on the west side of Dayton led to problems in later years, especially as the area took on a bad reputation.

The hospital's reputation wasn't helped by the fact that it was open to everyone. When other hospitals were confronted with homeless patients or those too poor to afford medical care, they weren't above shipping the patients to St. Elizabeth's. The hospital later became known as Franciscan Medical Center. Then, in 2000, the hospital shut its doors, as it could no longer afford operations.

Long before the hospital closed, stories existed about ghosts and haunted spots. Former employees remembered seeing the elevators moving on their own accord, opening or stopping on certain floors, as if someone pushed the buttons. Chris Woodyard discussed the hospital in *Haunted Ohio IV*. A former employee told the author about seeing dark shadows moving through the hospital and feeling cold spots.

Of all the employees, perhaps the security guards had it the worst. Even after the hospital shut down, these workers were still called upon to stand guard. Some reported seeing shadows and hearing voices. Former guards remember chasing people through the hospital, only to find no one. Was it the work of curious teens or something more sinister?

St. Elizabeth's is also home to the haunted spot known as the Nun's Room. A guard watching a security camera located at the nearby Dayton Heart

Montgomery County

Hospital spotted what looked like an explosion. Workers checked the room for any signs of an explosion or fire but didn't find a thing.

Guards working at the hospital also tell stories of a flowery perfume that is echoed by former hospital workers. The spot remains the same, with the scent nearly overpowering those in the area. The reason for the smell was never found, but legend claims that a former hospital worker always wore that scent. She smuggled drugs from the pharmacy for her boyfriend, but when she cut him off, he killed her.

One persistent rumor surrounding the hospital involves an odd occurrence in the atrium. This is the exact spot where the original hospital once stood. Rumor says that workers passed around a security tape, which captured a wheelchair slowly moving in circles on that spot, despite the lack of anyone around or any wind.

A reader of the website Forgotten Ohio shared stories told to her by her mother, a former worker at the hospital. Her mother claimed to hear the sounds of someone crying outside the pediatric unit, though she never found the source of the cries. Those who heard the sounds attribute them to a former nun who couldn't get over the dead children who once stayed in the unit.

I myself remembering visiting the hospital around 1998. A former boyfriend visited his grandfather, who was sent to the hospital after a heart attack and had surgery there. After visiting with his family, I wandered off by myself and felt a cold chill. I had the odd sensation of someone staring at me, but when I turned around, no one was there. I even felt the sensation of someone standing behind me, as if looking over my shoulder. It didn't surprise me when I learned that others had the same experiences in this old hospital.

Easily one of the most famous haunted spots in all of Dayton is Patterson's Tower. Also known as Witches' Tower, Frankenstein's Castle or Frankenstein's Tower, the building sits on Patterson Tower, just feet from the Dayton Community Golf Course. The MetroParks system now owns and maintains the structure, but even it can't stop the stories.

At one point, the tower was open to the public and served as a lookout point. Visitors climbed a metal staircase circling the interior of the building until they reached the top. During the 1960s, a group of teenagers was picnicking in the area when a sudden rainstorm hit. The teens ran for the

Patterson's Tower is practically hidden by trees, and police take effort to keep trespassers away. *Author's collection.*

safety of the tower and huddled together on the staircase. When lightning hit the tower, it sent electricity through the staircase, and all the teens were killed.

Another version of the story claimed that only two of the teens were killed and only then because they leaned against the metal railing, while the others stood at the bottom. The two teens on the staircase had their faces permanently etched into the stone. Another story claims that during storms, visitors can see the teens inside the tower. When lightning hits, it lights up their faces inside.

A less popular story told about the tower is that it was built on top of a burial ground, either a Civil War burial ground or a Native American burial ground. The story also claims the tower was built during the Civil War, which isn't possible. Maps and topography from that time give no mention of the tower. This also makes the story of it being a Civil War watchtower invalid. This legend says that a woman snuck onto the roof of the tower and killed herself. Supposedly she's now seen wandering around the roof, still wearing the black dress she wore on that fateful night and keeping an eye out for others.

As of 2010, new barriers were installed in front of the tower, blocking the turnoff we used to take the photograph on the previous page. Local legend claims that if you peer through the windows of the tower, you'll see the images of the teens still burned into the wall. The parks system keeps a close eye on the tower, and local police patrol the area frequently.

Frankenstein's Tower has other stories associated with it as well. One of the more common stories involves visitors who find ghostly orbs on photographs taken at the site. The website Forgotten Ohio lists stories from visitors who swear they saw figures moving at the top of the tower and a glowing stump behind the tower.

The tower is the source of much gossip and speculation from those living in the Dayton area. The stories date back to previous generations as well. Some claim that a ghostly car chased them down the twisty street out front and that a woman in white was sometimes seen standing outside the tower. According to some, the mysterious lady in white even chased them through the woods behind the tower.

On a personal note, I've visited Patterson's Tower dozens of times over the years and included it on quick "haunted Dayton tours" for out-of-town visitors. In all that time, the strangest or scariest thing we experienced was the owner of a house behind the tower flipping on her porch lights and screaming at us to go home.

On a trip there recently, I peered through the top windows and nearly jumped out of my skin. Suddenly, for the first time ever, I spotted what people kept talking about: those eyes looking back. The longer I stared, the less afraid I became. I ventured closer, keeping my eyes on the eyes and noticing that they never wavered. Then I saw what made my heart drop. Those ghostly eyes weren't actually eyes. They were, in fact, two cracks in the stone caused by the expanding and contracting of the stone. That said, there's still something odd and unsettling about the area, and it's well worth the trip.

Dayton is also home to the haunted Memorial Hall, which is home to a ghost named Drake. Memorial Hall dates back to 1909 and wasn't renovated until the 1950s. The building was originally meant to serve as a memorial to war veterans from Montgomery County. Drake worked as a custodian there during the 1960s or 1970s. Supposedly, he fell in the orchestra pit and died on site. He now likes to play with those in the building by flushing the toilets and turning the lights on and off. Some visitors have even heard him walking around on the catwalk.

Guests may also want to check out the Miami Chapel Elementary School or at least the vacant lot next door. Two stories exist about this ghost. One says that it takes the form of a half-man, half-horse, while others claim it's a woman sitting on top of a horse. Supposedly a cemetery once stood on the property but was moved during the 1960s, and the ghost is somehow connected to the original cemetery.

Montgomery County's Normandy Church in Kettering has a history that's almost as interesting as its ghost. Located on Alex-bell Road, the history of the property dates back to 1927. Richard H. Grant, a local businessman, built a cabin on the banks of Holes Creek and spent the weekends there with his family. Wanting a more permanent home, he purchased six connecting farms, totaling nearly eight hundred acres. He spent almost $1 million building a thirty-eight-room home over the course of three years.

Grant spent nearly as much money on the furnishings and design of the house. He brought in marble fireplaces, stained-glass windows and imported wood paneling from England that dated back to the 1600s. Inside the house, visitors saw eleven marble fireplaces and heavy concrete floors. The property consisted of multiple buildings and was named Normandy Falls, after Grant's hometown.

In 1955, the Ohio Miami Conference of the Evangelical United Brethren Church bought the fifteen acres of land that comprised the property, as well as all the buildings. It became known as the Normandy Evangelical United Brethren Church. The church still owns the property today. Grant himself last entered the building in 1957, when his funeral was held there, but his spirit might still remain.

The school, chapel and second-floor offices are the most haunted places in the church. The offices were once the bedroom of Mr. and Mrs. Grant, and some visitors have smelled her perfume lingering in the air. Stories are also told of strange noises.

One story told about the church relates to its spiral staircase. According to legend, one of the servants, a former caretaker or a relative attempted suicide by jumping from the staircase. Though she hit the stone floor, she

Montgomery County

The Old Courthouse in Dayton once had its own public gallows. *Courtesy of Derek Jensen.*

didn't die. Some claim she still haunts the building. A former janitor related a story to Forgotten Ohio claiming that he saw candles burning after blowing them out. Upon closer look, the flames were extinguished and clearly hadn't been burning. He also recounts a story about a co-worker hearing someone in the bathroom when it was empty.

Montgomery County once had its own public gallows, where offenders were hanged on site. The gallows still remain at the Old Courthouse, though they are obviously no longer used. People visiting the site claim to hear someone moaning in the building and hear footsteps moving up toward the judge's chambers.

The history of Dayton's Patterson Homestead dates back to 1804. The Montgomery County Historical Society now owns the building and offers tours of the grounds to the public. Thousands of schoolchildren have toured the property over the years, but few of those kids knew that the location was haunted.

The Patterson family lived on the property for a century, beginning in 1804. In 1810, Colonel Robert Patterson, who served in the Revolutionary

The Patterson Homestead is haunted by ghosts of those who once lived there. *Author's collection.*

War, and his wife, Elizabeth Lindsay Patterson, built the main house. Later additions were made, with the most recent dating back to 1850. Jefferson Patterson later donated the entire property to the city in 1953. He asked that they use the property as a memorial to his family, as well as a meeting center. The house was completely decked out with original antiques and furnishings that belonged to the Patterson family, many of which still remain there.

The third floor of the house is closed to the public, but visitors have reported seeing someone walking up to the area. As he's wearing military dress, some believe that he's a former member of the Patterson family. Those working at the property sometimes hear the sounds of kids laughing, even when it's empty. Workers also feel wind rushing by, and a psychic who visited the building once claimed to see a woman sitting in a rocking chair with a sick baby.

One of the more infamous stories involves workers seeing gingerbread cookies ripped off a drying line one night. The cookies were in place when they left and gone the next morning. Mrs. Patterson's former bedroom is also haunted and seems to always feel cold.

Montgomery County

One of the more haunted places in the Dayton area is Sinclair Community College. The history of the college dates back to 1887, when the Dayton YMCA offered several classes to local men. The class met in just two rooms but quickly outgrew its location. By 1910, it had moved farther downtown and began offering more classes.

Starting in 1929, the YMCA began offering both two- and four-year programs and housed several schools: the Dayton Technical School, Dayton YMCA School of Commerce, School of Liberal Arts and the Dayton Law School. The school finally received its name in 1959, becoming Sinclair College after an early secretary of the YMCA. Sinclair College became separate from the YMCA in 1959.

Officially renamed the Sinclair Community College in 1965, it continued growing. By the 1970s, the school needed even more space. A group of local architects designed the first seven buildings and had those built on its current location. Unfortunately, that may explain the ghosts at the college.

Part of the gallows and hanging field for Dayton were located underneath where the school now stands. The cafeteria sits on the exact spot where the gallows stood. At Blair Hall, students hear people talking and laughing when the building is empty. They also claim to feel someone pulling at them.

Blair Hall has other stories as well. The sounds of crying babies and cats in the walls are all heard, as are the sounds of people laughing and walking around. One student left in the building at night felt something rush by before darting out the revolving door in front of him, though he saw nothing.

Possibly the most famous story involves a security guard working at the college late one night. He saw the elevator reach his floor, the doors open and the chief of security walk out of the elevator and past him, as if walking to his office. The only problem was that the security chief had just died.

Sinclair also has a ghost that students dubbed Mr. Joshua. He's frequently been spotted in Building 12, which is where the United Color Press once stood. Legend claims that a worker in the old building died after getting his arms trapped in a press. He's always described as a white-haired, elderly gentleman wearing jeans. Workers and students have seen him wander through the halls and right through walls. The ghosts of another elderly man and his mule have also been seen, sometimes with Mr. Joshua. Some claim the ghosts are related to a roundhouse belonging to the railroad that once stood here. The railroad stored mules in the building until it was wiped out in the 1913 flood.

Locals also like to tell stories about Dayton's Stivers Middle School. Originally known as the Stivers Manual Training High School, it was completed in 1908. It was later known as Stivers High School and combined with the Patterson Co-Op High School before becoming a middle school. After renovations in the twenty-first century, students now have the option of moving to a different school after middle school or staying at Stivers through high school graduation.

When the school was first built, the designers added an athletic complex in the basement, complete with a swimming pool. In the 1930s, the school boarded up the pool and turned the space into classrooms. That's when the stories started. Weird things began happening, and students claimed it all related to a former teacher.

The story claims that the teacher was found dead in the swimming pool during the 1920s. She held a pointer in one hand and a locket in the other. The locket had two pictures, one of her mom and dad and the other of a mysterious man. The man was mysterious because his face was missing. A student who frequently helped the teacher disappeared around the same time, adding more mystery to the story.

After the teacher's death, the school closed off the swimming pool area. Workers placed plywood pieces over the swimming pool and covered it with linoleum. The rest of the athletic complex was converted into classrooms. The school gave little thought to the process, simply putting up new walls and laying down floor. Stairs in the basement once took kids to the locker rooms, but those stairs now end at walls.

A common story claims that teachers spotted a woman with white hair wandering through the halls of the school. One class in the school is constantly cold: the classroom with a trapdoor down to the basement area. Students and janitors have heard noises coming from the area. The school has a hard time getting teachers to stay in the classroom for very long. A cold breeze comes from the trapdoor, no matter what's done.

Supposedly there's a photograph floating around taken in the basement area. The photo shows a student standing in the swimming pool with a person in a hooded robe standing behind him. There are also stories about the ghost moving things, especially in the storage area on top of the swimming pool and in nearby classrooms.

Montgomery County

Of course, no look at haunted places in the Miami Valley area is complete without a look at the United States Air Force Museum. Author Chris Woodyard, who wrote the *Haunted Ohio* series, felt uneasy in the museum. "The place is full of death," she said. "There are dead guys looking over my shoulder whenever I stop to look at something."

Workers at the McCook Field began collecting artifacts in the 1920s. The artifacts were collected by the Engineering Division, which hoped to preserve those pieces for future generations. Wright Field became the home for the collections in the late 1920s, but the displays kept moving from building to building. It wasn't until 1954 that the museum received its first permanent home. Building 89 at Patterson Field began displaying the artifacts, often leaving them outside when space ran short. In 1971, the official museum building opened, giving the artifacts a true home. That's when the stories started.

The Black Maria, a Vietnam War airplane, is on display at the museum. The military used the plane for top-secret missions, and stories claim that the people who died on board never left. Hop-Along, which was used during the same era, saw quite a bit of action. A former pilot died in the helicopter, and his blood still stains the front seat. Workers have tried to scrub off the bloodstains, but to no avail. Janitors working in the museum claim to see the pilot sitting in the cockpit and trying to fly.

Stories are also told about the POW Exhibit. According to locals, anyone who visits the exhibit feels slightly sick or uneasy. Frederick Bock took over the helm of a flight during World War II and helped end the war when he dropped the bomb on Nagasaki. His plane, now called Bockscar, is on display at the museum. On the side of the plane are five painted figures: four black figures representing its test runs, and a red figure indicating its final run. That final run was dropping the atomic bomb on Nagasaki. Late at night, janitors have seen a small Asian boy running around the plane.

Another haunted World War II relic at the museum is the Strawberry Bitch. Legend claims that a gunner still haunts the plane and likes to play with the belly guns. The same ghost also hit a janitor late at night.

The United States Air Force Museum is home to a number of historic aircraft. *Courtesy of the USAF Museum Photo Archive.*

The Lady Be Good exhibit is rumored to be one of the worst in the museum. The Lady Be Good flew during World War II but crash-landed in the Libyan Desert. The plane got caught in a sandstorm, which caused an engine malfunction. Many visitors of the museum felt a heavy feeling or oppressive feeling as soon as they neared the plane.

Seven of the crew members died before one of the two remaining men went for help. He walked over one hundred miles before dying. Searchers looked valiantly for the plane, but it wasn't found until 1959. The plane was found perfectly preserved, with uniforms and rations in place, yet the crew had completely disappeared. Searchers later found the bodies of the crew members, along with a journal. Visitors feel uneasy when visiting the plane, and janitors have seen the crew members wandering through the museum.

Other stories are also told about the Air Force Museum. The Delta Dart is one of the only planes in the world that flew itself. During a training exercise, the plane went into a spin, forcing the pilot to escape. Not long after, the plane righted itself and somehow managed to fly for over nine miles before gently landing.

One of the more recent additions to the Air Force Museum, an Air Force One, also gives visitors an uneasy feeling. This particular Air Force One was used to transport President John F. Kennedy's body after his assassination. Some visitors felt the presence of a crying woman on the plane and even saw her. She typically takes the form of a pale-colored mist. Maybe she's connected to First Lady Jackie O., or maybe she's just one of the millions who mourned his death.

Generally speaking, the United States Air Force Museum isn't a site you want to visit after dark. Few janitors and custodians who worked there don't have a story. Most stories relate to dark figures they see from the corner of their eye who disappear when they turn. Full-body manifestations, footsteps and other weird noises are frequent occurrences. One late-night janitor even saw a mannequin turn and talk to him, while another saw the ghost of a former pilot standing on a plane and talking.

The University of Dayton started in 1850, when Father Leo Meyer purchased a tract of land known as Dewberry Farm from John Stuart. The land came complete with orchards, a few buildings, a large house and vineyards. The former farmhand building became the St. Mary's School for Boys, accepting fourteen students that first year. The school was also known as the St. Mary's

Institute, St. Mary's College and St. Mary's School. It wasn't until 1920 that the school became known as the University of Dayton. It became the first Roman Catholic university in the country to educate both men and women when it opened its doors to women in 1937. Today, it remains the biggest private university in the state.

When visiting the University of Dayton campus, stop by Liberty Hall. While it's now used as office space, the building was previously used as an infirmary. Hundreds of students and workers stayed there, and some believe the ghost of the hall is a former patient who passed on. The ghost is always described as having bad teeth and walking with a limp.

Another haunted building on the campus is the Theta Phi Alpha house. This sorority house is haunted by a male figure. Girls claim that no matter how much sleep they get, they always feel tired in the morning. Rooms stay cold at all times, lights flicker or turn on and off and heavy objects move on their own.

Not far away from the UD campus is Keifer Street. Rumor says that the railroad tracks that cross the street are haunted by a woman. She's described as having red hair and wearing a construction hat, but little else is known. Is she a true ghost or just a city worker trying to finish her job?

The Webster Elementary School is now permanently closed, but that might not stop its ghosts. In the girls' bathroom on the bottom floor, there sits a strange little door. Some claim it hides the body of a dead student. Legend says that a male student was playing and slipped on the recently washed floors. He smacked his head on the floor, dying instantly. A teacher or janitor moved his body behind the door to keep anyone from knowing what happened.

Near the University of Dayton campus is the haunted Woodland Cemetery. Students living in Marycrest, a dormitory, sometimes see a girl sitting next to a headstone in the cemetery. She's also been spotted by visitors. They always describe her as wearing a striped shirt, jeans and tennis shoes and having blonde hair. She's always seen crying and then disappears. Some visitors have even talked to the girl, not knowing she was a ghost.

Woodland Cemetery sits on a spot previously used as a farm. The City of Dayton purchased the land in 1841 specifically to create a rural cemetery. The city wanted a public cemetery that remained away from the residents. The location was close enough for citizens to visit loved ones but far enough away that they felt safe.

John Van Cleve was the pioneer behind the cemetery. The early settlers and pioneers of Dayton established a public cemetery at the corner of Main and Third Streets. However, as more people arrived in the town, buildings sprang up around the cemetery, blocking any possible expansion. With more citizens arriving, it became clear that the city needed a new cemetery.

Van Cleve was one of the trustees involved in picking the right location. He eventually decided on the area where the cemetery now sites. The name Woodland was chosen because of the abundance of trees. The park-like setting and atmosphere of the cemetery were well liked by residents. On weekends, families brought packed lunches and spent time in the cemetery, lunching on the grounds and sitting on benches. It's hard to imagine families doing this now, but at the time, it was the chance for the families to visit with loved ones. Kids died at a young age, and the tuberculosis and flu epidemics wiped out entire families. By the end of World War I, the death rate was waning, and the cemetery was used less for picnics and was less frequently visited.

Woodland Cemetery now looks much as it did then. The University of Dayton, South Park neighborhood and other neighborhoods circle the two hundred acres, but visitors still stop by every day. It's home to Lookout Point, the tallest point in the city, and is the final resting place of Erma Bombeck, Paul Laurence Dunbar, John H. Patterson and the Wright brothers. Its 1889 chapel, office and gateway are listed on the National Register of Historic Places, in part because of the original Tiffany windows.

Supposedly the girl's ghost is attached to a headstone that seems to glow blue. Others believe the two are unrelated. Legend says that the girl's father died and was buried in the cemetery. When she died unexpectedly, she was buried on the other side of the cemetery. She now sits by her dad's grave.

The other ghost at the cemetery is that of Johnny Morehouse. Morehouse was a local boy who never went anywhere without his pet dog. When he accidentally fell in the Miami & Erie Canal and died, he was buried in the cemetery. His dog kept visiting the grave and sitting next to it until he, too, eventually died.

In 1861, a new headstone was erected to honor both the boy and the dog. Guests now leave small toys and other items on the headstone. Today, visitors sometimes see the ghost of the little boy and his dog roaming through the cemetery. Students and locals living near the cemetery sometimes hear the sounds of a dog crying. In 2008, the head of the dog was broken off the tombstone, but it's now been replaced.

Montgomery County

There are some who claim the cemetery is also haunted by a ghost connected to Schantz, a famous figure in the city of Dayton who has a road and park named after him. A man told Forgotten Ohio that he was walking in the cemetery in the 1980s with a friend when they stopped to talk to a man by the Schantz grave. While talking to him, the man slowly started fading away until he disappeared completely.

Stories are also told about Paul Lawrence Dunbar. Dunbar grew up in Dayton and graduated from one of the city's schools. He leapt to fame with his poetry, but before he began earning money for his writing, he worked as an elevator operator downtown. He was just thirty-four when he died and was buried in the cemetery. Today, people occasionally see him sitting atop his tombstone, still reading his work to anyone who will listen.

Kettering Medical Center may not appear in many books on haunted places, but don't tell that to a former security guard who had his own ghostly experience there:

> *I was working there during the early 1980s, just after the birth of my daughter. I'd been a security guard for years at other places and never came across any ghosts. I hadn't heard anything about the hospital either. One night, I was making my rounds and heard someone walking around inside one of the locked rooms. I heard footsteps and it sounded like someone moving things around. Knowing no one was supposed to be inside, I listened for a minute and then got out my keys. I guess I just wanted to make sure that someone was really inside. When I opened the door, no one was there. The only way to get out of the room was through the front door where I stood, but no one came through it. I looked in every corner of that room and under every piece of furniture and no one was there. I still have no doubt that someone was in that room.*

Also in Kettering is the haunted Boggy Creek. The creek is practically hidden behind a large field, but it's the site of an odd event that happened during the 1950s. A group of young boys received permission from their parents to hold a sleepover near the creek. When the boys didn't come home the next morning, their parents walked up to the creek. The only sign ever found of the boys was a still burning campfire. It's said that they were eaten by the Boggy Creek Monster. Rumors still persist about a large creature running through the area.

Most ghost stories go back decades or even centuries, but not the one surrounding Swango Drive in Kettering. In the 1990s, a local man walked outside and promptly hanged himself from a tree on the side of the road. Ever since his death, locals have heard the sounds of someone moaning coming from that tree.

Another more recent ghost story from Kettering involves Candlewood Park. In 1988 or 1989, a young boy committed suicide in one of the bathrooms and now makes his presence known at night. The park also boasts the ghost of a murderer. Legend says that a man brutally killed three children in the park. Visitors sometimes report seeing a dark figure walking around the outskirts of the park or hearing the sounds of children screaming.

Dayton's Victoria Theater is haunted by several ghosts, the most famous being Vicky. Vicky was an actress who performed there during the 1920s. One night she went to her dressing room and was never seen again. There were only two exits from the building: out the dressing room window or down the stairs. Actors at the hotel have heard the sounds of her dress swishing and smelled her floral perfume. A local news station filmed at the theater in 1990 and captured the sounds of her dress moving.

The Victoria also has another ghost whom workers named Lucille. The story claims that Lucille was watching a performance on house left in one of the expensive privacy boxes with her chaperone. A man lured her chaperone away and then assaulted her. Even though she lived through it, some claim the effects of that night linger. A guest claimed to be slapped there, and many others felt uneasy or upset when sitting in the box.

The theater is also haunted by a man. Legend says that the man ventured into the theater one night and attached a knife to his seat. Then he threw himself on the chair and killed himself. When the backstage area still had curtains, actors and workers sometimes saw his face looking back.

A group of teenagers, complete with two chaperones, stayed overnight in the theater. They ran audiotapes that night and picked up a voice, believed to be that of Vicky or one of the other female spirits.

The Englewood Dam in Montgomery County is also rumored to be haunted, this one by the ghost of a little girl. The dam is relatively peaceful, with woods and a river surrounding it and walking trails in the nearby area. Those who have seen the ghost describe her as a shorter girl wearing a black cape, with pale skin. She's often seen near the trails but disappears as quickly as she appears.

Montgomery County

Near Englewood is the site known by locals as Patty's House. According to legend, several sisters once lived in the house. A relative of the girls killed Patty's sisters by hanging them from a tree. The hanging tree still stands on the property, though the only thing left of the house is the foundation. Locals claim to feel a cold air sweeping through the area and hear the sounds of the girls screaming.

Another version of the story comes from those who occasionally ride the trails surrounding the property. They claim to see the noose still hanging from the tree. The same people claim that the area has an eerie stillness surrounding it. Their version says that it was a man named Patty who was hanged from the tree and killed. Patty's House is located close to the Old National Trail Riding Center.

The Civil War saw a lot of young men lose their lives, and that pain still exists around Dayton, especially in places like the Germantown Cemetery. Germantown was originally known as German Township when it began in 1803 and was one of the only original townships in Montgomery County, dating back to before Ohio became a state.

Settlers from a small town in Pennsylvania moved to the area in 1804. Only one of the settlers spoke English; the rest spoke German. Phillip Gunckel became known as the founder because he was the only one capable of conversing with locals. He picked the location of the first gristmill and platted the town in 1814. The town slowly built up around the cigar and distillery industries, both of which are now gone.

The roots of the Germantown Cemetery date back to 1849, and some believe this Confederate soldier was one of the early residents. Visitors see the man wandering through the cemetery, dressed in his Confederate uniform.

Two stories exist as to why this soldier is so far away from home. One is that the man was a prisoner of war who died on the way to a northern POW camp and was buried there. The other story claims that he got separated from his men and died before they met up. He now wanders the cemetery, lost and trying to find his way home.

Germantown's Morningstar Road is haunted by a tragedy that befell a family years ago. Legend says that a young woman and her children lived in a house by the road. The house caught fire while the woman was outside and spread so fast that she couldn't get back inside. She ran to the street trying to find help, but none came, and her children perished in the fire.

Germantown Cemetery has an interesting mix of older headstones and more modern ones. *Author's collection.*

The mother ran into the woods surrounding the house but tripped over a tree root. She fell down and died when her neck broke. Travelers driving down the road sometimes glimpse a woman standing alongside the road, and some even claim that she waved to them. When they attempt to help, she disappears into the woods.

The woman's ghost is described as wearing an old-fashioned white nightgown with a high neck and having a long braid that reaches the middle of her back. She motions for travelers to follow her. Those who do watch as she disappears just as she reaches an old tree. Some believe the tree stands close to where her original house once stood.

Germantown locals know a longer version of the story. Supposedly it took place in the 1800s, when a young family lived in a house along Morningstar Road. The husband left his wife and four kids home alone as he went into town one night. His wife tucked the kids into bed upstairs and then went downstairs to finish some housework.

The night was warm, and she left the windows open to get air circulating and to cool off the house. Wind blew into the house, causing a kerosene light to engulf a curtain. The fire quickly spread through the front of the home, blocking off the only entrance to the upstairs and her children.

That didn't stop the woman from trying to get to them, and in her attempts, she was burned quite badly. She rushed from her home, trying to get to the road to find help. Blinded with panic, she ran right into a tree, and the force of the impact broke her neck. While the story of what happened dates back centuries, the first known report of the ghost only dates back to the 1970s.

Germantown has a haunted bridge with two separate stories. One story told about this old-fashioned steel bridge involves a truck driver. The driver lost control of his truck one night and fell over the side, dying when he landed in the creek below. Some claim that you can see the lights of the truck at night.

The other story is sadder and more popular. Legend says that two children were playing on the bridge one day when, for no reason, the little boy threw his sister over the side, killing her instantly. The story says that if you dare to venture under the bridge, you can hear her melodic voice singing. It's the exact same song she sang before her brother killed her.

CHAPTER 3

CHAMPAIGN COUNTY

Champaign County is fairly small, but that doesn't mean it lacks any ghosts or haunted locations. It even has its own crybaby bridge, this time with a slightly different story. The area is actually known as Crybaby Overpass because it's basically a small stretch that passes over the railroad tracks.

Legend says that a young mother carried her child to the overpass many years ago. She stood on the overpass, cradling her child until she heard the oncoming train. Then she jumped off, taking her baby with her. Visiting the site at midnight will reward you with the sounds of a train whistling, a baby crying and a woman screaming. Your car will die at exactly midnight if you're trying to cross the bridge and will refuse to start until the sounds pass. The original crybaby bridge was demolished and no longer exists.

The Evergreen Cemetery in St. Paris sits at the center of a great debate, all due to one tombstone. The McMorran family tombstone glows brightly, even during the dead of night. Thousands of people have visited the site over the years, some trying to find a reason for the glow. The most famous theory involves light being reflected from St. Paris and landing on the tombstone. Another theory claims that the headstone has some type of phosphorescent fungus attached, but no one knows the truth.

Like many towns in Ohio, St. Paris has its roots in the Native American culture. A group of white settlers stopped here in 1797, when the area was still home to local tribes. In 1831, a white settler named David Huffman arrived and decided to call the town New Paris. He changed the name after discovering that a New Paris, Ohio, already existed.

St. Paris has the haunted road known by locals as Lonesome Road. A farmer once owned the land surrounding the road, which started out as a simple trail through his farm. He was well known because he hated people on his property and wasn't above chasing visitors away. One day, he walked outside and hanged himself from a tree near his house.

The government took over ownership of the property, turning the simple trail into a full-fledged road. Over the years, numerous drivers have seen the man's ghost on the road. He's sometimes seen standing on the side of the road or directly in the middle, and some have even seen him slap their car as they passed. During the daylight hours, his eyes look as black as night, but they turn bright red when the sun goes down.

Also in St. Paris is the Trestle Bridge. A woman was somehow killed on the trestle when she was hit by a train, either by accident or suicide, depending on the storyteller. No matter when you visit the bridge, you might experience her ghost, especially the sounds of her walking across the bridge and her screams as the train neared closer. Many visitors have seen a mist moving across the bridge and felt cold spots on it.

Though he's most famous for his Illinois roots, President Abraham Lincoln is also connected to a ghost story from Urbana, Ohio. When the president was assassinated, his body moved through Ohio and through the center of Urbana. The conductor stopped the train on the tracks and let onlookers pay their respects for fifteen minutes.

Ever since the funeral, stories have existed about a haunted funeral procession. The ghostly train wanders down the track, even in locations where the tracks no longer exist. Smiling skeletons crew the train, which is covered in black fabric. The train causes clocks to stop, and when they do

Urbana had a charming, down-home feel at the turn of the century that still remains today. *Courtesy of the Library of Congress.*

start, they never show the correct time. It's said that the train still makes it regular stop in Urbana every year in April on the anniversary of its first stop. A less morbid version of the story claims that you can see the lights of the phantom train but never the train itself.

Urbana existed long before Lincoln's train passed through. William Ward, who founded the town, picked the name Urbana. From the moment it was established in 1805, it was chosen as the county seat of Champaign County. By 1840, the town was home to stores, newspapers, churches and over one thousand residents. By 1880, over six thousand people lived in town, due in part to the establishment of three railroads.

One of the more famous haunted spots in Urbana is a legend known as Hell House. Located on Clark Road, locals began referring to the site as Hell House because the house was falling in on itself, the result of years of neglect and exposure to the elements. Portions of the house were burned or missing, but few said anything about that. They said that the house looked that way because no one had ever truly lived there.

The owner of the house was working on the construction, hoping to give his family a new place to live. Unfortunately, his entire family was killed in a train accident not long before he finished. After completing the house, he walked outside and hanged himself. An oversized oak tree on the property is the site of his suicide. Locals say that if you visit, you might see a glimpse of the man still hanging from a noose in the yard. Others have heard odd noises coming from the long empty house.

According to the Ohio Exploration Society, the story of what happened at Hell House is slightly different. Once he finished the home, he set it on fire and then hanged himself. Another version of the story says that the entire house caught fire but somehow only a portion of it actually burned. Stories

Headstoners was kind enough to provide a photograph of Hell House taken before the building was demolished. *Courtesy of Headstoners and Megan-Marie Johnson.*

also claim that when you drive by the house, you can see the noose hanging from the branch he used. Like the crybaby bridge, Hell House no longer exists. The building was demolished by the city.

Urbana is home to a creepy road named Stoney Creek Road. Those driving down the road have heard the sounds of people talking and even someone screaming, though no one is ever around. Others have seen two ghosts appear on the side of the road before flying directly into cars. They then mysteriously disappear, just as they appeared.

Thackery is home to Hill Cemetery, haunted by a tragic story. The right-hand side of the cemetery, toward the back, is haunted by the ghost of a young girl who met her fateful end on the bridge. Legend says that a man grabbed the girl during the 1970s, raping her in the cemetery before putting an end to her life. Visitors to the cemetery have seen the girl standing in the area where the event occurred.

Bigfoot lives in Ohio, at least according to the legends surrounding Cedar Bog. The entire area is contained by a chain-link fence, taller than some believe it should be. Legend says that a Bigfoot lived in Cedar Bog and killed multiple people during the 1970s, 1980s or 1990s. The fence was installed to protect those living in the area. The official stance is that it keeps deer from getting through the bog and onto the road. That hasn't stopped hundreds of people from feeling uncomfortable when passing by and feeling watched, by someone or something. There are even stories from people who heard the sounds of a person screaming beyond the fence.

Urbana University began in 1850 as part of the Swedenborgian Church. Several members of the church gained a charter from the state to start the school. Originally, the classes took place in a small room downtown, and students referred to the school as the Urbana Seminary. The first students were elementary and high school students.

In 1853, the school finished its first building, Bailey Hall, and began offering college classes the following year. The school closed down at the start of the Civil War and only opened its doors once the war ended. In 1911, the school decided to stop offering elementary school classes, and the high school closed in 1928. By 1968, the school was offering four-year degrees under the name Urbana College. It wasn't until 1985 that it became known as Urbana University.

The railroad tracks near North Hall are also haunted. Some claim to smell a rose-scented perfume belonging to a woman who died on the tracks. Others claim that a ghostly train still runs along the track. Within North Hall itself, students have nicknamed the ghost Rose. The hallways and rooms in the building occasionally begin smelling like rose or another heavily floral-scented perfume. Perhaps Rose sometimes makes her way over to Brown Hall, which also has a female spirit.

One of the most haunted buildings on the college campus is Brown Hall, which has a ghost that students believe is female. She sticks to the top floors. The ghost moves things around, plays with the lights and makes odd noises. Supposedly the students have seen pieces of a broken tombstone on the stairs and footprints leading up the stairs. There are also stories of things moving, odd noises and weird lights on the top floors.

King's Creek in Champaign County is equally haunted. A Shawnee general living in the area was dubbed "king" by a group of white settlers because he wore fancy clothes and seemed respected by others in his tribe. The general and his men attacked the white men but ran into problems when their main gun failed.

The story behind the ghost is even more interesting. Along the bank of the creek sits a honey locust tree that's much taller and bigger than the surrounding trees. Supposedly the ghost of the general sits on the top branches of the trees, nearly hidden by the leaves. Walk by his spot too close at night and he'll scream in warning.

CHAPTER 4
BUTLER COUNTY

Medlar View Elementary School is a fairly new and modern school near Middletown. Standing outside and listening to the sounds of kids playing and laughing, it's hard to imagine it has a ghost. Legend claims that one of the construction workers murdered a girl in the fourth-grade bathroom. She now appears in the mirror of the bathroom, complete with blood pouring down the glass.

Arguably the most famous haunted site in Middletown is the Sorg Opera House. The building dates back to 1891 and was used for opera until 1915. At that point, the theater began showing movies. As with all theaters during the early twentieth century, the theater had two separate balconies: one for whites and one for "coloreds." The second balcony was hidden, though it still remains. The theater changed back into a stage theater in 1985.

The most popular ghost story told about the theater involves Paul J. Sorg. He built the theater for his wife because she loved opera music and dramatic performances. One of his portraits still hangs in the lobby of the theater, and guests have claimed that he looks exactly the same as he did in the picture. Actors and workers have also heard him walking around the catwalks and the backstage area.

Legend also claims that a former patron keeps returning to his seat. The African American man keeps going back to his original seat in the second balcony, turning up for every show. It's especially odd given that the balcony

Above: Medlar View Elementary School looks almost too new to have its own ghost. *Author's collection.*

Left: Paul Sorg was the original founder of the Sorg Opera House in Middletown. *Courtesy of Wikimedia Commons, illustrator unknown.*

is now blocked so he can't see the stage. Theater workers occasionally drop off a program for him, especially before a new show.

Another story is told about a woman wearing a red dress. Janitors working in the building at night hear a woman's voice singing softly. They sometimes find the woman sitting and staring at herself in a mirror, singing as she applies makeup. She abruptly disappears as soon as they see her.

The 1960s and 1970s were a dangerous time to be gay, even during the free love era. One of the girls' gym teachers at Stephen Vail Middle School hid her secret, but other teachers at the school discovered it. They made her life a living hell, and one day, she couldn't take anymore. The teacher escaped into the locker room, hid in one of the stalls and killed herself. Students and teachers have sometimes seen her ghost running laps or heard her playing in the gym and slamming locker doors.

Middletown's Woodside Cemetery is haunted by something that no longer exists. Around 1850 or 1860, a group of five men passed through Middletown on their run from the law after robbing a bank. A group of locals banded together, captured the men and hanged them from a tree in the cemetery. Not long after, locals began seeing the ghosts of the five men swinging from the same tree. Cemetery officials tore down the tree, but people kept seeing the same image.

The Sorg Opera House looks just as grand today as it did originally. *Courtesy of user Darth Bengal, via Flickr.*

Fairfield has its roots in the late 1800s, when Judge John Cleves Symmes purchased land in the area after a single visit. A friend who had served in the Revolutionary War with him informed him of the area. He eventually bought over 300,000 acres of land in 1794. Revolutionary War veterans quickly arrived in the area but found settling difficult.

The local tribes in the area were unresponsive to the white men, and fights frequently broke out. Men who settled on the land found themselves

This image shows Middletown as it appeared in the 1950s. *Courtesy of user Nyttend, via Wikimedia Commons.*

attacked and forced to move. The men weren't accustomed to the harsh Ohio winters and had problems battling the cold temperatures and icy and snowy conditions. The lack of food and problems in growing food created even more problems.

The problems went even further than that, as small villages began popping up. Those who needed help often couldn't afford to pay for that help. Those who needed food and assistance from an employer found it difficult to find anyone hiring. Eventually, the settlers decided to band together to survive the harsh conditions. Men watched for enemies, and families helped support each other by growing their own food.

Two main roads eventually passed through town, as did railroads and interurban electric lines. By 1898, the town even had its own streetcars. The two main roads later became known as State Route 4 and United States Route 127. This only helped the town continue to grow.

In 1953, the Hamilton Chamber of Commerce began looking at property in Fairfield for possible annexation. At the time, it was still known as Fairfield Township, but that would soon change. A group of citizens, worried about what would happen, banded together and had the township officially declared a village in 1954.

Butler County has its own haunted sites, ranging from a haunted college to a ghostly pizza shop. First is the story that locals refer to as the Screaming Bridge. Located on Maud Hughes Road, on the outskirts of Fairfield, this bridge is haunted by a young girl. The young woman and her boyfriend were driving home one night and fighting the whole way. As they crossed the bridge, she decided to jump out rather than spend another moment in his company. She fell off the side of the bridge, dying when she hit the river. It's said that if you stop and wait on the bridge, you'll hear the sounds of their fatal last fight.

Stories are also told about the railroad tracks visible from the bridge. Several people have seen an odd light coming from the tracks, similar to a train light but not as large or bright. Others have seen a ghostly train coming down the railroad tracks without making any noise.

The Fort Hamilton Hughes Memorial Hospital is haunted by the ghost of its namesake, Mr. Hughes. The man continually walks around the hospital checking up on patients. Nurses have seen him in the ICU area, looking through windows. Another nurse reported hearing moans coming from an empty hospital room.

Butler County

Fairfield is also home to the haunted Fairfield Middle School. According to legend, a student at the school did something he shouldn't and was afraid of his parents finding out but also afraid of what the principal would do. He walked into the bathroom and was found dead there the next morning. The mirror lay broken in pieces and he sat cut in one of the stalls.

The severity of the cuts and the fact that he was literally in pieces made it difficult to determine if he killed himself or someone else did it. Teachers working in the school late at night have heard the sounds of a boy screaming in the bathroom. Students feel uneasy in the bathroom, as if someone is watching them. Additionally, stories say that visitors still see stains on the floor from his blood.

A small creek behind the Fairfield Bowling Lanes is haunted by two ghosts. Supposedly a young woman was walking with her son along the creek when they were brutally murdered by a killer moving through the area. The two wear old-fashioned clothing, dating back to the late eighteenth or early nineteenth century.

The ghosts of young kids are typically hard for many people to handle. It's even harder when the ghosts are of children who died when their deaths were avoidable. Such is the case at the Fairfield YMCA. Locals say that a six-year-old girl was swimming in the pool, and while the lifeguard was busy with other things, she drowned. She now haunts the area where she once played.

Also in Fairfield is the haunted second-floor call center at Hammacher Schlemmer. For years, workers have reported hearing odd things in the building, usually when only a few people are left there. They hear someone typing at one of the desks, but when they investigate, the noise suddenly stops.

Hamilton, which once tried to take over Fairfield, has its own share of ghosts. Originally, plans called for the town to be named Fairfield, but when it began in 1794, it was actually known as Fort Hamilton. General Arthur St. Clair named the site after Alexander Hamilton and established the site as an army post. It was incorporated in 1810, only to lose the title a few years later. Along with Rossville, it was finally incorporated again in 1827. A few years later, the two cities separated, only to reconnect in 1854.

Hamilton grew up around different industries, including the iron industry. Immigrants settled in the area, taking jobs in the plants. At one point, the town had a large Jewish community. Hamilton's history also had a dark side. During the 1920s, a number of gangsters purchased homes in the city, and even John Dillinger visited.

The area along Pershing Avenue was originally known as Wood Street. This is where guests found a long line of houses with prostitutes ready and willing. During the 1940s, active soldiers were prohibited from visiting the city, solely because of its reputation. In addition to the prostitution, the city was known for drinking and illegal gambling. Despite its unusual history, Hamilton continued to grow and thrive.

The Butler County Fairgrounds in Hamilton has an odd and unusual ghost. A man once walked into one of the bathrooms hiding a gun under his clothes. He promptly shot himself in the head, killing himself instantly. Dozens of people have seen the ghost of a bleeding man walking around the fairgrounds late at night, with blood covering his clothes.

The Butler County Treasurer's Office in Hamilton is haunted by a former security guard. While working there in the 1860s, he was killed by men trying to rob the building. They killed him with an overdose of ether and left him hanging from a rafter, hoping people would assume he killed himself. A famous story says that the guard appeared in 1893 on the face of a clock and made it chime twenty-one times. Though he hasn't been seen since, people still like to talk about the building.

Driving down Hamilton's Princeton Road is creepy enough, even if you don't know the stories. A portion of the road has seen dozens of crashes over the years, including a number of fatal accidents. A woman who died in one of those crashes sometimes materializes at the site, warning others of what happened. Some even claim that she'll climb in your car for one last drive…if you're willing.

The Ruppert House in Hamilton is haunted by a gruesome story that reminds everyone that you can't always be safe, even from your own family. Even today, it ranks as the biggest mass murder committed by a family on a family. To make the story even worse, it happened in 1975, on Easter.

The small house on 635 Minor Avenue doesn't look like much, but once you know what happened, you'll never look at it the same way again. James Ruppert was the stereotypical "nice guy"; the one no one realizes has ulterior motives until it's too late. He collected guns and knew how to shoot them, but no one thought he would ever actually use them.

Butler County

James was forty-one years old and still living in his mother Charity's house. That Easter day, they hosted a celebration, inviting over his brother Leonard and the man's family. All told, there were twelve people in the house, including James's sister-in-law, Alma, and his eight nieces and nephews, including a four-year-old and a seventeen-year-old.

The family played outside for some time, looking for Easter eggs before coming back inside. As they started working on dinner, James walked out with four guns, including a .357 and a rifle. He walked through the house carefully, killing the adults first and then the children. Investigators discovered that he shot them once to stun them and keep them from fighting back and then a second time to kill them.

None of the family members fought back. Police found only a trashcan tipped over as a sign of what happened. They also discovered that one of his nieces made it to the back door and opened it slightly just before he shot her. After waiting three hours, he finally called the police.

At trial, the defense presented James as the poor, mistreated one in the family. They emphasized his failures professionally and personally. They revealed that a former fiancée dumped him and another girlfriend left him for his brother, and they eventually married. James began expressing signs of paranoia, thinking his brother was messing with his car and that somehow he had convinced their mother to kick him out.

The prosecution painted a much different picture. They showed that Ruppert was practicing with his guns in the days before the murders and even asked about buying a silencer. He also told a woman he knew that he needed to deal with his mother. Though the defense fought for an insanity plea, it was rejected when the court learned that he would inherit the life insurance policies and properties of all the victims as their remaining heir.

The court ruled that he was guilty of the murders of his brother and mom and not guilty by reason of insanity for the other murders. He was sentenced to two consecutive life sentences in prison. Ruppert came up for parole in 1995 but was turned down. He remains incarcerated at the Allen Correctional Institute and won't come up for parole again until 2035.

A public auction was held at the house, selling off all the contents and the house to the public. The new owner added new carpeting and made renovations to the house, but even through it all, people and former occupants still tell stories.

A former occupant of the house told his story to the website Forgotten Ohio. He was one of the first people to live in the house following Ruppert's slaughter. According to the writer, his mother once saw a dark shadow wandering through the hall and a light turn on though no one was in the hall. There are other stories told about residents hearing footsteps walking through the house and hearing noises inside, as well as bloodstains that won't come off.

Miami University is located in Oxford, but a campus of the school in Hamilton is haunted. Mosler Hall is rumored to be haunted, with the ghostly activity stuck on the fourth floor.

Employees of the old Wal-Mart in Oxford believed that it, too, was haunted. Workers frequently lost their keys, only to have them turn up in the exact spot where they went missing. Store computers left idling had random drawings on the screen, and the electronic doors often failed. The store closed in the 2000s, when a new superstore opened in the city.

According to local legend, the Reily Pizza Parlor in Reily is haunted by a poltergeist. Late at night, long after the restaurant is closed, motorists have seen the lights turning on and off.

Wehr Road Cemetery in Trenton is haunted by a murder that occurred on the property. Legend says that the man responsible for the cemetery was killed one night by a man carrying a hatchet. Even in death, he still wants to take care of the cemetery. Drive by late at night and you might see him holding the hatchet and chasing away pesky kids. Some also claim to hear him hitting a mausoleum with the hatchet, and if you look closely, you'll actually see evidence of chips in the wall.

The history of Miami University relates to George Washington. After becoming president, he decided that a school should be located in this area. Judge John Cleves Symmes owned the land in this area, but part of the deal involved with the purchase stated that he must use part of the land for a school. Once Ohio became a state, surveyors were sent with the sole purpose of identifying an area for the school to be located. By 1809, legislature called for the formation of Miami University, originally known as College Township. The area was renamed Oxford.

Work on the school stopped because of the War of 1812, and Cincinnati attempted to move the school. The hope was that the money used to fund the school would go to a Cincinnati school. Finally, in 1818, the grammar school opened, but it only lasted five years. In 1824, the school picked Robert

Hamilton Bishop as its president and started running classes for all twenty students. Originally, the school offered just one program, and students had to take courses on Roman history, Latin, Greek, geography and algebra.

The following year, the school started the English Scientific Department, which offered mathematics, economics and languages. By 1827, the school had its own weekly newspaper, which later became known as the *Miami Student* and is still published today. Soon after, the school started its farmers' college and theological studies department.

The 1930s were a difficult time for Miami. The school started its first fraternity but also saw eleven students get expelled. A former employee moved to Cincinnati College, where he spoke out against Miami. The president resigned, and eventually, enrollment started dropping. The school closed in 1873, owing money to others, and used the site as a grammar school.

It took twelve years for the school to reopen, after fixing up the older buildings and paying back its debts. Slowly the school began offering more classes and adding sports. The school became well known with the graduation of its first African American student and eventually rented rooms from the nearby college for women, Oxford College, to make room for more students. Andrew Carnegie even donated money to the school for a new library. In 1928, Miami University and Oxford College merged, creating a much larger school.

The campus of Miami University has several haunted spots. "Diamond" Judge Elam Fisher was a well-known presence in the Oxford area. A diamond-shaped necklace that he wore led to his eventual nickname, and

Miami's campus looks unchanged at times. *Courtesy of the Historic American Buildings Survey/Library of Commons.*

Fisher Hall was named for him. It was one of the most haunted buildings on campus until the school tore it down to make room for a conference center.

Fisher loved playing pranks on those living in the buildings. At one point, a bust of him was moved to another floor and kept moving, making a diamond pattern with its movements. The bust then moved in different ways, creating the shape of his initials before it finally disappeared. Those who lived there also claimed he stole a variety of things from people in the building, usually around the theater.

Fisher Hall was also home to the ghost of a former student named Ronald Tammen. Tammen's roommate arrived back to their room on April 19, 1953, and found no sign of the young man. Despite the cold outside, his coat lay draped across the chair, and his books were left sitting open. He was never seen or heard from again. Even though the building is gone, some students believe that the ghosts still live within the new conference center.

Helen Peabody likes to haunt the building named after her. Originally named Seminary Hall, Peabody Hall dates back to 1855. In 1861 and again in 1871, the building caught fire and was rebuilt by the school. Peabody founded the Western Seminary. Western Seminary and Miami University merged in 1974, and the school remodeled the building but kept the name. Students claim to see things move and hear weird noises. Room 210 is supposedly the most haunted. A former student committed suicide in the room, and it was also the site of another suicide.

Reid Hall was haunted by a murder that occurred in the building in 1959. On May 9 of that year, Resident Advisor Roger Sayles attempted to break up a fight between two students. One of the students shot and killed Sayles during the altercation. He ran from the building and into nearby Ogden Hall before turning the gun on himself. Students claimed to see a bloody handprint on the wall exactly where Sayles fell after being shot. Stories of weird noises were also told. Miami University tore down the building in 2007.

There's also Wilson Hall, which was used as a tuberculosis hospital prior to the college taking over. The ghosts of patients who died there now haunt the building. Students have heard the sounds of people moaning and found furniture moved or tipped over. Students also claim to feel someone watching them and have items moved to different places while they're sleeping.

Butler County

A more generic story is told about a woman wearing a black dress. Students believe that she was once a student at the school, and they see her standing in line at the cafeteria. Dozens of students have seen her over the years, but all they remember is her dress and the sad expression on her face.

Just outside of Oxford is Buckley Road, which is home to several different versions of the same story. Buckley Road runs off 732 and is the exact spot where a bicyclist was killed. A car came around the corner quickly, striking him down. If you pull onto Buckley Road and turn toward 732 before flashing your lights, legend says that you'll see the cyclist take the form of a white light coming down the road.

Oxford also has a haunted house with a famous story that's attached to the Buckley Road legend. The story has three separate versions, depending on who tells it. Located just down the road is an abandoned house that's falling down on itself. The house has been abandoned since one fateful night.

The house was once lived in by a young family. The daughter began dating a man whom her parents hated, in part because of his motorcycle. He'd ride up the driveway and tear off with their precious girl attached to the back. Her parents demanded she stop seeing him, and she agreed, only to meet him in secret.

He would drive past the house, park down the street and then turn with his lights flashing the house. He'd flash the lights three times, and she would sneak out to meet him. They made plans to meet and run away together, getting away from her parents. One night, he drove down the road, flashed his lights and waited for her. Despite the pouring rain, she slipped outside and started across the property. She fell and broke her neck on her way to meet him.

An alternate version of the story claims that the young man couldn't control his motorcycle due to the pouring rain outside. He crashed and skidded into a nearby field, decapitating himself in the process. She ran outside, found his body and killed herself.

The third version of the story claims that the two were in love but he went away to serve his country in the war, most likely World War II, though the war varies. Though she agreed to remain faithful, she fell for another man while her lover was gone. He arrived home to find her in the other man's arms and crashed his motorcycle while driving away. Yet another version claims that she fell for another man when her parents forbid them from seeing each other. In this story, the young lover also died while trying to get away after seeing them together.

No matter which version of the story it is, the ghostly legend part remains the same. It's said that if you pull your car into the driveway of the home and flash your lights three times, you'll see the headlights of the motorcycle coming down the road. Some claim that the house was torn down or fell down, but the driveway still exists.

The Ghosts of Ohio website uncovered yet another version of the Oxford late-night rider. In this version, the girl's parents had no qualms about her love interest. The young woman was waiting at home for her parents to get back when she noticed a car pull up the driveway. It sat outside, with the driver honking the horn and flicking his lights. In a panic, she called her boyfriend, who rushed over on his motorcycle. He took a curve too fast and died when he wrecked.

The legend also claims that the man inside the car was a serial rapist wreaking havoc on the Oxford area. Legend says that you must drive to the exact house where the girl lived, blink your lights three times and honk your horn three times. You'll then see a ghostly motorcycle coming toward you, following the same path it took that night, including the fatal crash.

The website draws connections between this story and that of the Elmore ghost rider. The Ghosts of Ohio researched the story and discovered that the story has existed for decades. It has received different versions of the story that put the true house in five different locations in Oxford.

The Elmore ghost rider story, found on that site and many others, shares a number of similarities to the Oxford legend. The story says that a young man left his girlfriend behind while he went to serve in the military. The first thing he did after coming home was meet his parents and then drive his motorcycle over to his girlfriend's house. When he saw the curtain moving in her bedroom window, he peeked inside and found her with another man. He drove off in a fury, sliding off the road and right into a barbed wire fence, which decapitated him.

The legend says that you must visit the bridge near where he died on the anniversary of his death, March 21. Sit on the bridge on that night, flash your lights three times and you'll see the ghost of the motorcycle rider still trying to make his way home.

Butler County

A small stretch of U.S. 27 in Butler County became known as Highway to Heaven, in part because of the numerous deaths that occurred there over the years. One story claims that a ghostly form on a motorcycle comes racing down the road and either disappears or flies over the car. An even odder story about this stretch of road comes from a local:

> *When I was a kid, my mom worked for the emergency medical team. As soon as we were old enough to drive, she warned us about the dangerous roads around Warren and Butler Counties, but seemed the most worried about us driving down 27. She told us about a few of the accidents she saw there. Back then, we didn't know the Highway to Heaven story, but it fits with a picture she showed us. It was taken after a bad accident when a preacher crashed his car. His head was thrown through the steering wheel or something because there was blood everywhere. You could actually see brain matter in the car. Everything moved, but right on the passenger seat was his Bible, still sitting where he left it when he got in the car. She told us that after they moved his body and moved the Bible, the seat underneath was perfectly clear. It was like the Bible didn't budge, even during that huge accident. Maybe it was because the good old preacher was drinking and driving?*

CHAPTER 5
WARREN COUNTY

Middletown borders two counties—Butler and Warren—and has enough ghosts for both counties. The city's Jefferson Elementary School no longer exists but was once the site of some ghostly activity, as witnessed by former students and teachers. Students claim that the school was built on the site of a former Native American burial ground. The school was torn down in 2003.

One of the most common stories told centered on the school gym. Teachers, students and janitors heard the sounds of kids playing inside. When they opened the doors, the gym was always empty. There were also stories told about the ghost of a little girl seen in the hallways.

Middletown's Woodside Cemetery has a ghost related to something no longer there. Once upon a time, a large tree stood in the cemetery. Locals referred to it as the lynching tree or the hanging tree for the nefarious acts that took place there. Visitors to the cemetery kept seeing the image of people hanging from the tree, which led to a group cutting down the tree. It didn't work, though, as visitors still see the phantom image of the tree, complete with the ghostly hanging victims.

Tecumseh is one of the most famous Native American leaders in history, but his brother Tenskwatwa is the one haunting Fiddler's Green Road around the Mount Saint Joseph Cemetery. According to legend, a fiddler decided to sell his soul to the devil, hoping to play the fiddle better than anyone around. After the deal expired, he sat in the cemetery and played the fiddle, waiting for death. Tenskwatwa appeared and somehow traded spots with the fiddler. A blinding flash occurred in the cemetery, and Tenskwatwa was left tied to the cemetery.

Located in Madison Township is Gunkel's Mill Bridge, which lets Old Franklin–Trenton Road go across Elk Creek Bridge. Though it no longer exists, there was once a small log cabin sitting near the bridge. Known as the tavern, an older couple ran it for a number of years. Locals claimed that the couple had a large amount of money hidden somewhere on their property.

The couple was older, and it wasn't surprising when the wife died. What was surprising was when two strangers breezed into town, telling the husband that they were lost relatives of his wife. They started running the tavern, and when the husband stopped showing his face, they told people that he had gone back to his hometown in Maine.

Not long after the husband disappeared, so, too, did the men. The tavern sat empty for a number of years, with no owner and no one to take care of it. A huge storm caused the creek to rise, washing out the bridge. Those passing through the area heard sounds of people screaming and moaning inside the abandoned tavern.

Years after the storm, a new couple purchased the land, including the tavern. They tore down the building and found a gruesome discovery. There in the cellar was a room with a hastily thrown together wall, with a man's skeleton inside. His body still had chains in place from where the men chained him inside. The new owners buried the man's body, and the screams stopped.

Located on Route 122 in West Middletown are the remains of a coffin factory. Thomas Wilson partnered with Charles Miller in the 1830s to create the factory. Near the house was a cemetery, which made operating easy. Wilson stayed in the back, crafting the coffins and caskets, while Miller took care of the funeral arrangements.

Locals claim that the coffin factory is haunted by the ghosts of those who were buried there. Next to the factory is an old shed where Wilson did some of his work. Stories of ghosts moving between the shed and the cemetery are often told. Some claim that the ghosts are taking their last steps in this world.

Warren County, Ohio, is home to a number of small towns, including many with their own ghost stories, such as Carlisle. Carlisle was once known as the Jersey Settlement. During the early part of the eighteenth century, a large number of settlers from New Jersey arrived in the area. One of the earliest residents, James Taposcott, donated a small tract of land to the Baptist Church, which in turn built the Tapscott Church in his honor. The church still exists today, though it isn't used for religious ceremonies. The town continued to grow when two railroads passed through the area.

George B. Castle, who was well known in the railroad industry, purchased a large portion of the area and divided the land into plats. One of those plats was given to the community and was eventually used for the town hall. Carlisle built its first store in 1932 and officially became a city in 1958.

The small town of Carlisle has several apartment complexes, including the Carlisle Park Apartments. Right across the street from the apartments is a dead tree with deformed branches. Look for a bike path, and the tree is right beside it. The woods surrounding the trees are home to odd noises, dark shadows and what looks and sounds like creatures running. Though the tree is long dead, it still appears to grow. On a recent visit, it was nearly impossible to find the actual tree. During the warmer months of spring and summer, the surrounding trees grow large enough to nearly cover the demon tree.

Also in Carlisle is Zech Road, sometimes referred to as Miamisburg-Zech Road. Right along the street is a small barn that's barely standing and shows signs of a fire. Legend says that two children were playing inside the barn when it caught fire and they were trapped inside. Those passing through the area have heard the sounds of children playing and giggling. The barn sits on the stretch of road between Miamisburg and Carlisle.

Another small town in the area is Franklin. William C. Schenck founded the settlement in 1796 and named it after Benjamin Franklin. It was incorporated in the early 1800s and officially named a city in 1951. Warren County named four post offices in 1805, including the Franklin Post Office. The original building still stands on River Street and is open for tours.

Franklin is known for John Brown, a horse breeder who lived in the city during the 1930s. Though he went bankrupt and quit breeding, other breeders continued working. One horse named Belmont was bred in the city and became fairly well known. The city also built the Garbage Recycling Plant, which recycled metals and paper products.

Warren County

Morningstar Road has an unsettling feeling at almost all hours of the day. *Author's collection.*

An interesting story told about Franklin involves Alan Stratman, who owned a restaurant called Jonathans Café. Stratman told investigators that he was a bookmaker for ballplayer Pete Rose. His testimony and records were used in the investigation into Rose's betting. The former restaurant was later demolished, and a gas station now sits on the property.

Morningstar Road, which has its own stories, crosses into parts of Franklin. The sharp curves and turns of the road are difficult to navigate, and locals claim that dozens of people have died or crashed there over the years. Reports of a dark figure standing on the side of the road are heard, and nearly all claim that the figure fades into the trees when spotted. Orbs are also reported along the side of the road.

Warren County is perhaps best known for being the home to King's Island. The park opened in 1972, operated by Taft Broadcasting. The company built the park as a replacement for Coney Island. Coney Island, which was the prominent park at the time, couldn't expand any further and experienced flooding from the river. The park originally featured just a few rides, the Eiffel Tower and a small area for kids.

In the coming years, the park added other features, including the International Restaurant and Wild Animal Safari. The park became home to the College Football Hall of Fame and started work on the Beast in the 1970s. The park eventually opened Hanna-Barbara Land, catering to children and complete with smaller rides. It also opened Winterfest, a winter-long event. The park eventually added a water park and shut down some of the less popular rides.

The amusement park has several ghosts of its own. One is that of a high school senior who died on the Eiffel Tower. Johnny visited the park on May 13, 1983, for a Grad Night celebration, a chance for high school seniors to let loose. He climbed into the elevator shaft and was killed by the cables inside. The park moved the cables to the woods by the Beast, but that hasn't slowed down Tower Johnny, who is frequently seen in the park.

Johnny actually did die at the park, but the park claims he died while inside a roped-off area of the Eiffel Tower. Apparently he climbed over the ropes used to block off the area. Some claim that the cables were placed inside the woods by the Beast, which led to that ride becoming haunted. Others claim to see Johnny staring from the top of the Eiffel Tower, a forlorn look on his face. Still others claim that Johnny haunts the fountain in front of the Eiffel Tower. The reports always include the same description of the teenage boy, sitting and staring off into space.

King's Island has its own campground, and located right beside it is a small cemetery. The ghost of a little girl buried in the cemetery haunts the amusement park. She has appeared to tram drivers late at night and likes playing in the water park. No one knows her name, but many believe that she may have died in the park. Others believe she died long before the park existed on the property.

The little girl is usually described as wearing a blue dress and having long, blonde hair. Guests who saw the girl guess she's six to eight years old. Tram drivers sometimes claim they had to stop suddenly to avoid hitting the girl, who then disappears. Some claim the little girl is upset because all the children are having fun while she's stuck in her own world.

She's certainly not the only child haunting the park. Another ghost is usually referred to as "Racer Boy" because he's often spotted near the Racer roller coasters. He's always described as wearing all white and is never seen

Warren County

The Eiffel Tower replica at King's Island was where a teenage boy died during his graduation celebration. *Courtesy of user Knife-Thrower, via Wikimedia Commons.*

King's Island's own cemetery is rumored to be haunted. *Courtesy of the Forgotten Ohio website.*

in other areas of the park. Workers at the park report hearing guests ask about the boy, wondering why he's alone after dark.

Several ghosts also haunt individual rides, such as the ghost who died on the Octopus ride. Two of the more famous ghosts are those of the Beast and the White Water Canyon ride. Workers gave the ghost at White Water Canyon the nickname of Woody. Workers stuck on Tower 2 at night hear the sounds of rocks hitting the tower. Woody is rumored to be a visitor who died on the ride, though there's no record of this happening.

Those riding the Beast at night sometimes see glowing red eyes along the track near the woods. Some believe that it's the ghost of a person who died on the ride, though records show that no one died on the Beast.

Another tragic event that occurred at the theme park happened in 1992. On June 9, a man climbed into the pond outside the Viking Ship ride to rescue his hat, which the wind blew off. Two other men jumped in to rescue him and were electrocuted. A woman who had too much to drink climbed onto the Flight Commander ride. Supposedly, she didn't strap herself in properly and fell to her death. As the two events happened on the same day, it became known as Black Sunday.

King's Island also has its share of local legends that aren't true, including those that started with the originals. For example, some claim that the electrocution story involved a woman, and these people swear that their version is the true story. They claim that a woman accidentally fell out of the Viking Ship. A park worker rushed to her aid and was electrocuted. They claim that his ghost now haunts the park.

Another story involves the Flight Commander ride. Some claim that a small boy died when he wasn't strapped in properly and fell from the ride. This story is sometimes connected to the story of the ghostly boy in white. Yet another story involves the Flying Eagle. Legend says that a young mother put her two kids on board the ride and stood to one side. As she was watching her kids take off, a wire came loose from the ride and decapitated her. Both of these stories aren't true, and the Flight Commander ride was dismantled.

The first real death at King's Island has long been forgotten, in part because the attraction where he died no longer exists. During the 1970s, the park had its own Wild Animal Safari, also known as the Safari Park. Guests sat on board a tram as it ran through a wild animal park. In 1976, one of the riders decided to explore and climbed out of the tram. He died when a lion attacked him. In

Warren County

The Peters Cartridge Company retains its unique characteristics. *Courtesy of R. Myers.*

an alternative version of the story, he accidentally fell from the tram. Either way, it gives you a lot to think about on your next visit to the park.

The Peters Cartridge Company in King's Mills is also haunted. The factory was built in the 1860s to help craft ammunition for Union soldiers. Morgan's Raiders targeted the factory during their infamous trip through Ohio but somehow managed to miss it. The building closed in 1944, only to reopen and close under the Remington name. It opened again as part of Columbia Records, making vinyl records. This lasted only until the 1950s, and then the building closed again.

In 2002, the building was used as part of the setting for a horror movie. *The Factory*, as it was eventually released, told the story of a group of reality show contestants who are murdered. Those who worked on the film had some weird experiences. The most common was the sound of footsteps walking around the upper floors when no one was there. One worker even claimed that a ghost spoke to her and refused to enter the room for the rest of the shoot.

Peters Cartridge Company is home to some ghostly activity. Many claim the ghosts relate to workers who died there as the result of industrial accidents and explosions. At least three men were killed there in 1940 alone. At night, people hear the sounds of footsteps from uninhabited floors, and some walking along the nearby Little Miami Trail have even seen ghostly figures inside the top floors.

Left: Some claim this photo, originally posted on the Forgotten Ohio website, shows a ghostly figure standing in the window. *Courtesy of the Forgotten Ohio website.*

Below: The Golden Lamb is one of the oldest inns in the state. *Courtesy of E.F. Schrand and A.R. Arend.*

Another famously haunted site in Warren County is Lebanon's the Golden Lamb. For a number of years, a log building sat in this location. Run by Jonas Seaman, it provided public entertainment for locals. The business brought in a number of customers when the county courthouse opened in 1815.

Warren County

Seaman closed down the shop when his debts grew too big, and Ichabod Corwin tore down the log structure, building a large brick building there. It's the same building that exists today. Robert Jones and his wife, Virginia, ran the hotel during the Great Depression by selling junk and used furniture. Among the famous people who stayed at the hotel were Daniel Webster, Charles Dickens, Harriet Beecher Stowe and even Mark Twain.

The Golden Lamb is home to the ghost of a girl named Sarah. Supposedly she was the niece of manager Isaac Stubbs. As his niece became an adult, some believe the ghost is actually that of a girl named Eliza Clay. She and her father, Henry, were staying in the hotel in 1825 when she got sick and died. The staff gave the ghost her own room, dubbing it Sarah's Room. She makes herself known with noises and by knocking things off the walls.

Also at the Golden Lamb is the ghost of Charles R. Sherman. Sherman, who was an Ohio Supreme Court justice, died there in 1829. Guests have reported seeing a pale, older man standing in the hallways. The building is smoke-free, but that hasn't stopped Sherman from making his presence known with one of his cigars.

It's not surprising that Lebanon has a few haunted sites, given its history. Just after the end of the American Revolutionary War, settlers began arriving in Lebanon. A surveyor arrived in the area and laid out Main Street and Broadway, with one hundred lots for houses. By 1807, Lebanon had its own newspaper, the *Western Star*, a jail and a courthouse.

Alfred Holbrook arrived in town in 1855 and created the Southwestern Normal School, which became known across the country and eventually ran its own university. Resident Mary Ann Klingling donated $40,000 to the city in her will, provided that the city use the money to build a site for orphaned and abandoned children. It took the town nearly twenty years to raise the necessary funds to make the dream happen, but in 1886, the Mary Haven Home for Children opened.

This haunted spot in Lebanon is also known as the Orphans' Asylum and Children's Home, and some put its date of completion at 1879. This is where orphaned children and poor children were sent to live, as well as sick children and those with mental problems. One of the poor boys living there committed suicide by hanging himself in the barn on the property. He still haunts the property, as do other children who died there. The Warren County Juvenile Court now owns, maintains and operates the building.

The building is occasionally referred to as Mary Haven's Boys Group Home. Those outside the building sometimes see children peeking through the windows, especially in the attic and on the third floor. They seem to be staring into the yard, as if still wanting to play outside. Multiple people have seen full-body apparitions of both kids and adults in the building, especially in the bedrooms and on the stairs, as well as in the old recreation room.

Lebanon's Glendower State Memorial is also haunted. This Greek Revival-style house dates back to the 1850s. A volunteer working at the site heard a small group walking up to the front door one day and went to wait for the group. After a few moments, she looked outside and found no one there. The sounds of a fire burning are also heard, though no one uses the fireplace today and it's cold and dark. There are also stories of people hearing others inside, laughing, talking and singing, as if attending a fancy party. When they walk inside or peer through the windows, the building is dark and empty.

Located at 101 East Main Street in Mason is a dark brown house called the Chokolate Morel. The building was originally used as a private home, and that's where a tragedy befell the McClung family. In the early twentieth century, the wife, Rebecca, was discovered dead in her bedroom upstairs. Immediately following the murder, her husband, John, was arrested and charged with her murder, in part because blood coated his clothing and body. While he walked away from the arrest, Rebecca lingered on. Those walking by sometimes see a woman standing in the window of the room where she was murdered.

The odd thing was that locals rarely ever saw the woman prior to her death. While she was beautiful, her husband hated sharing her and was so jealous of other men looking at her that he kept her practically imprisoned in the house.

John met the young Rebecca and they married, despite the fact that he was fourteen years her senior. He was a jealous and spiteful man, frequently accusing her of cheating on him, even if she hadn't spoken to another man. Rebecca eventually stopped leaving the house, holing herself up inside for thirty years, choosing to watch people passing by on the street rather than going out and enjoying life.

Oddly enough, when the murder happened, they weren't the owners of the home. A Mrs. Baysore purchased the property from the couple but allowed them to live in an apartment on the second floor. It was she who heard the screams on that April morning in 1901. When she heard someone on the stairs, she ran up to the apartment and found Rebecca badly beaten and covered in blood. It was she who called the police and a doctor.

The doctor who arrived on the scene did so at six o'clock in the morning and found a hellish scene. He discovered that someone had crushed her skull, probably with an ash log. He also discovered that she had hidden over the blankets at one point, trying to hide from the attack. He was also the one who noticed the blood on John's clothing and hands.

Rebecca's husband had a much different story for authorities. He claimed that he woke and left the apartment at 4:00 a.m., as he needed to take care of the animals and do other chores around the farm. When he returned, he found her dead. He also told authorities that the blood on his clothes and hands came from a cut on his wrist. As evidence, he showed the scar from the cut.

His attorney argued that unknown assailants killed Rebecca. At trial, the lawyer claimed that the couple kept money around their home hidden inside wood barrels. As more proof of the attack, they showed other cases of wealthy older couples getting robbed or murdered in the early mornings. Whether it was true, John walked away from the trial a free man. It's worth noting that some believed he tried to make the jury feel that he was senile or insane. During the trial, he sat in the courtroom, eyes closed and talking to himself for much of the day.

Locals believed that John got off easy, perhaps because he was well known and wealthy. Regardless, he didn't get off that easily and actually spent two years in an insane asylum after the trial. Upon release, he lived with his sister, and when he died in 1904, she buried him right beside Rebecca. Oddly enough, his own brother committed a similar act. Elmer McClung loaded up his family, took them to another location and returned to their home. After setting the house on fire, he killed himself.

More recently, the building played host to the Chokolate Morel restaurant, which has since closed. Employees at the restaurant heard doors slam and other odd noises. In one strange incident, a glass bottle fell from a tall shelf and broke. When an employee went to clean up the mess, the soda was cleaned up and the glass pieces were stacked as if someone had already helped.

Pam Kennedy and her partner, Dave, began renovation work on the building in 2002 before opening it as a restaurant. In the room near the left-hand side of the stairs, guests report seeing a black man. The most frequently told story about him relates to the Underground Railroad.

Originally, a different house stood on this site, and it was believed to be part of the Underground Railroad. A tunnel supposedly runs across Main Street. Some claim that the man was hiding in the tunnels and died before he could escape. When the new house was built on the site, he started haunting it.

The room on the right-hand side of the stairs is also haunted, or at least Chris Woodyard, author of the *Haunted Ohio* books, believes so. During a visit to the building, she claimed to feel the presence of a man in this empty room. She also believes that the ghost of a sad woman haunts the server's pantry on the second floor.

According to locals, John killed Rebecca with a piece of wood taken from beside the fireplace. The bloodstains from her murder stayed on the house for years and refused to come clean. While the building is now vacant, some locals still claim to see odd lights moving through the building and hear voices and other sounds coming from inside.

Rebecca is not above leaving her ill-fated bedroom, at least for brief stretches of time. Near the building is the Rose Hill Cemetery, where both Rebecca and John were buried. A groundskeeper saw a woman dressed in old-fashioned black clothing stop by the grave site. Days later, he saw an image of Rebecca and realized it was the same woman. A woman in black is also sometimes seen in the basement area.

Rose Hill Cemetery also has its own vanishing hitchhiker urban legend. The story says that a young girl was on her way to meet her boyfriend for prom when she was hit by a car and killed. She now stands outside the cemetery gates, trying to find someone willing to drive her to her boyfriend. She disappears long before reaching her long lost lover.

Warren County has a stretch of road referred to as Spook Hollow or Spook's Hollow. It is dangerous, with a sharp curve followed by a tiny bridge. One night, a group of teenagers was driving down the road when they veered off the road. The car crashed into the railing of the bridge, which gave way, sending them into the water below. One of the riders, a young girl, was decapitated in the accident, and while they searched, locals never found her body.

Legend says that if you stand on the bridge at exactly midnight or stop your car there, you can see her head floating in the water. Another version of the story claims that if you drive over the bridge, you'll hear a thumping sound as her head falls onto the roof of your car.

Salem Cemetery in Springboro has a wide variety of ghosts. An unnamed home in Springboro once served as a stop on the Underground Railroad. A former owner woke one night to find a black man standing at the foot of her bed. He motioned to her with his hands, trying to ask her for help. It's believed that the man died accidentally in the house.

The Underground Railroad is an important part of Springboro's history. Numerous houses and buildings throughout the city still have traces of escape tunnels and hiding spots. It's thought that the Quakers who originally helped settle the town provided much of the help for the escaped slaves, as they were staunchly against slavery.

The Pioneer Village in Caesar's Creek is also haunted. The Pioneer Village has a number of buildings and log cabins that show visitors what an old settlement looked like. The buildings are a mixture of originals moved from other areas of the state. One of the houses is called Levi Lukens and dates back to 1807. The ghost who haunts the building is called Uncle Bob, and he died in the 1940s.

Waynesville is called the most haunted town in Ohio, and for good reason. It boasts its own haunted tour of the city every year around Halloween simply to share the top haunted sites with visitors. Samuel Heighway was a British immigrant who arrived in America in 1791. He built a cabin near the Little Miami River and surveyed the area, platting the land for the town of Waynesville.

Heighway and two other men purchased thirty thousand acres near the Little Miami River. John Cleves Symmes, who owned thousands of acres of land, agreed to the sale. The men named the town Waynesville, after General Anthony Wayne. Heighway then arranged for the shipment of goods to the area. It's obvious that the men didn't know what to expect and were unprepared for the Ohio winter. Once the Ohio River froze over, they had to stop their trip to Waynesville and settle down for the winter. Much of their goods sank to the bottom of the river when their boat was damaged by the ice.

Heighway began selling off the land he had purchased in the hopes of enticing new residents. All buyers agreed to build homes on their newly purchased property. He later platted the land for the town and became one of the first settlers, even running his own store and a mill. Heighway and his wife eventually moved to Clark County and were living in Cincinnati when he eventually died.

Problems arose in Waynesville when it was discovered that citizens didn't actually own their land. Symmes had sold land that wasn't included in his plots, and the citizens bought land that technically belonged to the government. David Faulkner purchased the land in 1807 and resold the land to the citizens.

Waynesville later rose to prominence because it was antislavery and a free territory. James Smith, a slave owner from Virginia, visited the area. He was so moved by his trip that he sold all his slaves, purchased land in the area and moved his family there. Elizabeth Smith eventually founded the Waynesville Methodist Church. By the end of the eighteenth century, the Society of Friends, or Quakers, began settling in the area because of the antislavery views.

The Quaker Meeting House, built in 1805, was used until 1811, when a brick structure replaced the wooden building. By the 1850s, the area was home to over seven hundred residents. The Waynesville National Bank appeared in 1875. The town was home to several well-known residents, including John Evans, who later founded the University of Denver, Northwestern University, Mercy Hospital and the Indiana Hospital for the Insane.

It's hard to be certain of the exact history of Waynesville because the city experienced a massive fire in 1900. The fire destroyed almost every building on Main Street's west side, including the village offices. It also destroyed the village records. The village implemented a new series of ordinances and laws.

The Quaker Meeting House was built by Quakers who settled in Waynesville because of its antislavery views. *Courtesy of the Library of Congress.*

Warren County

One haunted site in Waynesville is a building that dates to the 1890s and was used as a private club. Visitors frequently felt someone watching them, even when they were alone, and often heard the sounds of people walking around upstairs, though the floor is heavily carpeted. A spot inside the building supposedly has fresh bloodstains, and one of the ghosts likes to drink glasses of water left sitting out. The ghost or ghosts also bangs on the walls occasionally and has thrown things across the room.

The Crosswick Monster is a Waynesville legend that dates back to the 1880s, when two boys claimed to see it. Ed and Joe Lynch saw the monster rise up out of the water and attack them while fishing. They claimed the monster looked like an oversized snake with back legs and small arms. Three men, including a reverend, saw the monster for themselves when they went to help the boys. They watched in stunned disbelief as the creature climbed into a tree.

When stories spread about the monster, a band of local men decided to go out to the tree and capture or kill the creature. The sight of the monster climbing from the tree scared the men so bad that many of them ran off. The men who remained watched as the creature ran off and went through a hole in the ground. They blew up the hole, but that didn't stop the monster. Reports of it later turned up in Caesar's Creek Shaker Swamp.

Walk down the street outside the Angel of the Garden Tea Room and you might catch a glimpse of a man staring down from an upstairs window. During renovations of the house in 1950, the owners found bones hidden upstairs. Some believe the ghost belongs to those bones, even though he had a proper burial.

The Hammel House in Waynesville is a restaurant serving homemade food and locally produced pies. It also serves as a hotel and has its own ghosts. Workers have seen ghostly figures inside the building, heard odd noises and seen things moving. The Hammel House Inn appears on the haunted walking tour of Waynesville every year.

The Waynesville Area Culture and Heritage Center is haunted by the ghost of an old schoolteacher. Many people have seen her on the stairs inside. The building was previously used as the Waynesville Friends Boarding School, and some believe she was a teacher there.

When Waynesville needed a firehouse, a local man donated land. Though he died in 1982, he still likes to walk around the property keeping an eye on things. The man lived in a house right beside the firehouse and frequently came over for visits, even having his own key to the firehouse. Firefighters have heard the side door open and someone walk upstairs or heard someone walk downstairs and out the side door, taking the same path the man once did.

Odd things go on at the Quaker Meeting House. Originally, it had a separate building that served as the kitchen, but that hasn't stopped a ghost from cooking and baking, rattling pans and other things that no longer exist. Stories of a woman wearing old-fashioned clothes and sitting in the window are also told. Locals notice that she always sits next to or holds a candle. There are also stories told by people who heard someone playing an organ.

In 1820, the Stetson House was built in Waynesville. John Stetson, who invented the famous hat of the same name, used the home for his sister Louisa. She lived there until passing away from tuberculosis in 1879. It's believed that he may have passed her the fatal disease during a visit in the 1860s.

Many people have seen the ghost of a woman with dark brown hair inside the house. It's believed to be a former schoolteacher named Lila Benham, or even Louisa herself. Benham was a teacher in town who lived in the house during the early twentieth century. Some of the stories told about the house include smelling gingerbread baking, though there's not a kitchen in the house. Owners have problems using mirrors as well, as they keep falling off the walls. Maybe Louisa doesn't want to be reminded that she should move on.

Miami House may be haunted by the ghost of a murder victim. A wealthy traveling salesman stopped at the inn one night and took a room. The next day, the owner of the inn filled in a well on the property, and no one ever saw the salesman again. A spirit photographer took an image there that seems to show a hand pointing at the shop owner.

One of the antique shops on High Street is haunted by the ghost of a former store owner. One night, the man closed his shop, walked up the stairs and hanged himself from the banister. He still takes his fateful last steps today. Those working in the shop have heard the sound of someone walking up the stairs and then heard the sound of his body falling over the side.

Warren County

The Satterthwaite House is named for former resident Elizabeth Lynton Satterthwaite, who died in the house in 1879. Many believe the ghost is Elizabeth herself. Former residents claim the ghost plays tricks, such as hiding needed items. Others have felt someone touching them and seen rocking chairs moving, as if someone is sitting there.

Waynesville also has a sad and slightly tragic story, that of Charity Lynch. Isaiah and Charity Lynch moved to Waynesville in 1805 from South Carolina. They began building a house for their family, but when Isaiah died unexpectedly, Charity was at a loss. She eventually sent her children away, hoping to reconnect with her family soon. It wasn't until 1818 that she sent for her children. By then, she was living in Springboro, and one of her children wouldn't make the trip.

Her youngest daughter, Mary, died while waiting for her mother in Cincinnati. The little girl was sad and confused and couldn't understand why her mother had sent her away. The family didn't have money to pay funeral costs, so the little girl was placed in a potter's field. Charity searched for her grave, but to no avail. Eventually, she moved back to Waynesville, where she moved into a house close to the Quaker Cemetery.

Many believe that Charity is the ghost at this house. Others believe that it's May Wright, a librarian who owned the house during the late 1910s. She held séances in the house and had an interest in the supernatural. Doors in a cabinet came open on their own, and many women who lived in the house heard the voice of a woman talking.

CHAPTER 6
DARKE COUNTY

Darke County is best known for the town of Greenville, which has several haunted sites. General Anthony Wayne settled the area in 1793, naming it Fort Greene Ville after Nathanael Greene. Wayne was here until 1794, using it as a supply depot and a staging area, as well as a winter encampment. The men planned on marching against tribes in the area.

Native American tribes sent leaders to the fort in the hopes of creating peace treaties. The Treaty of Greenville was signed in 1795 and brought peace to both settlers and Native Americans. The agreement called for the northern land to be given to the tribes, but war broke out again when white settlers continued moving north.

The town officially became known as Greenville in 1808 and, by 1840, was home to eight hundred citizens. Just a few years later, the town had its own shops, newspaper, churches and a flour mill. Bear's Mill is a flour mill in Greenville that dates back to 1832. President Monroe gave the land to Major George Adams to reward him for his service to the United States military. Gabriel Baer later built the grinding mill on the site in 1849. In 1977, the mill was added to the National Register of Historic Places. It's still used today, grinding out rye flour, whole wheat flour and cornmeal.

The ghost of the mill is described as an older man who looks like a farmer. While he doesn't always take on the form of a figure, he presents himself in different ways. Some have heard his footsteps wandering around the upper floors of the mill.

Baer's Mill is one of the oldest buildings in Greenville. *Courtesy of user R.P. Piper, via Wikimedia Commons.*

Also in Greenville is the haunted McMecham Road. Rumor says that this land was once the site of a Native American burial ground. Rather than memorialize the men and women buried there or move the bodies, it was decided to build the road right on top of the burial ground. Stories are told about dark, shadowy figures walking along the road at night. Some even claim that the figures chased after them.

Memorial Hall in Greenville has the spirit of a former custodian. The man worked in the building for years until he fell from a ladder. Apparently, he slipped when changing a burned-out light bulb. Weird noises, including footsteps, are heard, and workers blame the odd occurrences on the former janitor.

Greenville's West Water Street is haunted by the ghost of a Native American girl who once lived in the area. Men stationed at Fort Greenville grabbed the girl one day and sexually assaulted her before throwing her back into the wilderness. Worried about her tribe throwing her out, the girl killed herself, and the tribe had her body buried under a large boulder that now sits on the street. Locals believe her spirit haunts the road and surrounding homes.

Arcanum is home to several ghosts, one of which is found in a local park. Behind the park is an area locals refer to as "Dead Man's Path" because the ghost of a man is seen there. He's usually spotted lying on the ground, facedown.

Staff at the Arcanum Public Library tell stories of a ghostly man in black. He's usually seen on the stairs or the landing and is always dressed in black clothing.

Main Street in Arcanum has an old-fashioned feel, with buildings from the 1920s and earlier, lining either side of the road. In the upstairs of one of these stores is a female ghost. She's usually seen looking out the window and holding a baby in her arms. She wears a calico dress in a pale shade of gray and has a bored expression on her face.

CHAPTER 7
SHELBY COUNTY

Shelby County is best known for the ghosts in Sidney, but nearby Lockington has its own haunted tale. Locals claim that dozens of people have committed suicide at the Lockington Dam and that the ghosts of those deaths still haunt the area. If you visit the dam on the anniversary of any suicide, you'll see the poor soul reenacting his or her final moments.

John Loughlin was a famous citizen even before he built Bonnyconnellan Castle in Sidney. Loughlin moved to Sidney about 1878 and created the Sidney School Furniture Company. At one point, the company was one of the largest manufactures of desks for schools in the United States. He spent $10,000 to build the Bonnyconnellan Castle, making it look similar to one in Cork County, Ireland, where he once lived. Loughlin handpicked every piece of furniture, decoration and accessory in the house; many of those pieces were made by workers in Europe and shipped to Sidney.

Loughlin sold his company in 1895 but retained ownership of the castle. In 1904, the German American Bank went under, losing Loughlin a large sum of money. The bank's creditors retained ownership of the property and sold it to Colonel J.B. Tucker in 1907. Tucker used the former desk factory to make bicycle rims. Stanley Bryan purchased the castle and owned it until the 1920s, also running the Venice Chocolate Company. He lost most of his money after the stock market crash of 1929. Dr. Austin Edwards owned the building for several years, as did Major Charles Price. In the 1950s, the Morris family turned the castle into a retirement home.

Bonnyconnellan Castle as it appeared in the 1920s. Mike Kramer, who passed along the photo, was the grandson of Stanly Bryan, and his mother was born in the castle. *Courtesy of Mike Kramer.*

Rose Loewer eventually bought the castle from the Morris family but refused to stay there, perhaps because of the ghost stories. It then became a boardinghouse, with multiple people and families living in the building and renting individual rooms. Victor Frump and his wife later purchased the castle and attempted to renovate it. In 1979, Tom and Vivian Jutte purchased the building and set about renovating the property.

In 1996, Kim and Dean Shepherd purchased the property. At one point, it was used as a bed-and-breakfast. The couple also completed restoration work on the property but never finished their plans. The bank sued the couple for removing original woodwork and fixtures from the property. In 2007, the value of the property dropped to $90,000 from $250,000 due to the damage inside. It sold for just $64,000 at a sheriff's auction in 2000. It is still awaiting its much-needed restoration work.

Throughout the years, past owners reported odd occurrences at the property. Local legend claims that one family raced from the building in the middle of the night, much like the scene in the movie *Poltergeist*. Strange noises coming from the basement led them to run away. One owner reported hearing kids laughing and playing in the basement, as if they were holding an unseen party.

On the stair landing, there was once a wedding dress on display. Dozens of visitors to the house spotted a man standing in the area and staring at the dress. His only distinguishing feature was the blue uniform he wore. With the interior now gone, who knows if he still remains? Perhaps he's moved on, still looking for the woman who once wore that dress.

The city of Sidney started out as just seventy acres of land. Locals named the city after Sir Phillip Sidney, a British government official. Charles Starretty donated a portion of land that would later become Sidney, Shelby County's seat. Sidney continued to grow in the 1820s and again in the 1850s, thanks to the Miami-Erie Canal and the growth of the railroads.

When Bridgeview Middle School first opened in Sidney, it opened its doors for high school students in the city. The Presbyterian Cemetery, which stood on the land, had to be moved, which seemed to happen fairly quickly. The basement of the school had an odd opening that led to tunnels underneath the school. Those who glimpsed in the tunnels were surprised to see the caskets of formerly buried locals who somehow were never moved.

Legend claims that one of the school janitors became brave and decided to explore the tunnels, never to be seen again. Those souls who attempted to look for him were met with the sounds of keys jangling. Even in the 2000s, students and teachers claimed to see a dark figure wandering around the tunnels, as if he was still trying to find his way out. The school was torn down in 2005.

The Tri-County Community Action Commission is rumored to be haunted by the ghost of a former worker who died in the building. Workers saw items move across the room on their own and experienced problems with electrical items, including calculators.

Shelby County has yet another crybaby bridge, but the story has a twist associated with the local community. The story involves an Amish family crossing the bridge in their horse and buggy. Inside was the baby in a small carriage. They hit a bump in the road, causing the child to fall out and roll into the creek, where it drowned. In another version of the story, they were walking across the bridge and the baby fell out of its carriage and drowned. Both stories end with the baby's cries heard at midnight.

Sidney's Bridgeview Elementary School was demolished in the mid-2000s, but numerous people experienced ghosts inside prior to its destruction. A janitor in the school decided to check on the furnace, and several people saw him head into the basement. He was never seen again. Teachers and students heard his keys jingling and went looking for him, but they never found a trace of him.

There's also an interesting story circulating about Sidney's Monumental Building. Nearly seven hundred young men from Shelby County were killed in the Civil War, compared to just seventeen during the Vietnam Conflict. Women saw their husbands, sons and lovers leave, never knowing if those men would come home. Following the end of the Civil War, locals met to determine how best to honor those poor souls.

It wasn't until 1867 that they finally came up with a plan. Several men got together and acquired the local building known as Carey Hall. They sold lottery tickets, with the winner gaining the building. They raised just over $9,000 before the plan stalled yet again. In 1871, a committee was created to bring a war memorial to the city.

The committee purchased the site where Monumental Building would soon stand in 1873. In 1875, the builders laid down the cornerstone of the building, dedicating it to the soldiers from Shelby County who died in the war. The building was home to several stores, a library and even had its own opera hall on the third floor.

By the 1940s, though, the building was in trouble. Longtime residents left, including the fire department and library. In the 1990s, the building had a surge when the city manager helped gain a community development block grant, which allowed for restoration and repairs. The story behind this building is what makes the story worthwhile.

City manager Bill Barlow woke one night to hear the words of Sergeant Fair, a soldier from the Civil War. The soldier asked him kindly to save the building. Barlow immediately set about getting the funding. Perhaps the soldier is happy with his work, as people have spotted a ghostly figure moving around the balcony area of the court.

Shelby County

The Shelby County Historical Society sits inside the William A. Ross Historical Center. It's also known as the William Haslup Home, named after its builder. It was built in 1902, and after Haslup died in 1912, it was used as a funeral home. Historical society workers claim the building is haunted. Pictures fall from the walls, and workers sometimes hear footsteps when no one else is around.

A man working in the building heard someone walking around upstairs while he was working in the downstairs area. He ventured upstairs, unsure of what he might find. As he made his way up, he heard a loud crash, which turned out to be an oversized calendar. Despite the fact that the building was empty, the calendar somehow flew from one wall and landed right in the middle of the room.

Author Chris Woodyard visited another haunted building in Sidney, an unnamed brownstone-style house. She heard the sounds of a baby crying while walking up the stairs to the second and third floors. Upon looking out a window, she saw the ghost of a woman holding a baby in her hands. She then experienced what felt like a woman being marched down the stairs and out the front door. Though it was the same woman she had seen earlier, the woman no longer had her baby.

CHAPTER 8

CLARK COUNTY

Clark County is home to Springfield and several ghosts and haunted spots. James Demint is credited with founding Springfield. He arrived and started the town in 1801. By 1818, Champaign County, Madison County and Greene County were split up to form Clark County. Springfield was picked as the county seat.

Springfield grew up around National Road, or Route 40. The road led from Ohio into Indiana and let travelers easily reach Richmond, Indiana. Originally known as an industrialist town, Springfield later became known as "Home City" for its number of lodges that built homes for orphaned kids. Glessner Manufacturing Company also started in the city and later became part of Navistar International.

The 4-H Club also began in Springfield, though it was originally known as the Boys' and Girls' Agricultural Club. Starting in 1902, the club offered food and agriculture projects for children under the age of fifteen. Springfield is also known for two racial events. One, which occurred in 1904, was extremely dark. Richard Dixon, an African American man, was arrested on the charge of killing a white police officer. A lynch mob broke into the jail, shot Dixon and then hanged his body in downtown Springfield.

The mob continued to shoot the man's lifeless body before turning on other black residents. The mob stormed the predominantly black area of town and set multiple fires. Two years later, residents once again set fire to the black area of town. Yet in 1966, Springfield elected Robert Henry as their mayor. He became the first African American mayor in the history of the United States.

Clark County

The George Rogers Clark Park in Clark County's own Springfield has a long history. General George Rogers Clark, for whom the park was named, led a battle on the site where the park now sits. The Miami, Wyandot, Delaware and Shawnee tribes were all involved. Yet the haunting at this park is connected to a small house located inside the park.

Known as the Daniel Hertzler House, the site was home to Hertzler himself. Hertzler lived and worked in the area, running a sawmill along Buck Creek and helping to open the first private bank in Clark County. On October 16, 1867, several men broke into the house. One of the men grabbed his wife and held her. When he released her, she ran to get help and carried their child to a neighbor. The police found Hertzler the next morning, dead from a gunshot wound to his leg. They theorized that the men were looking for government bonds and cash that he kept on hand.

The most common story told about the house is that the ghostly image of a man peers from the windows. Perhaps Hertzler is unhappy about what happened to his murderer. Of the four men present that night, two were acquitted of his murder. The other two men were placed in a jail cell next to a female prisoner. Police left her cell door open because she was sick, letting her walk around the jail. The men cut a hole between the two cells, walked out and were never seen again.

This is not the only haunted house in Springfield; so, too, is the Pennsylvania House, which is open to the public. The house was once called the Inn at the End of National Road for its proximity to National Road, now known as Route 40. Built in 1840, it originally served as a tavern and inn and today exists as a museum maintained by the Daughters of the American Revolution.

The ghosts reenact their travels across the National Road, complete with their entrance into the former tavern. Long after sunset, lucky witnesses see a long line of wooden wagons slowly make their way down the road before pulling into the yard of the Pennsylvania House, which was once the parking lot. Some even hear a few ghostly cries from the people inside the wagons and hear the gentle clopping sound of horse hooves on the ground.

The park now offers tours of the park, but don't expect to hear stories about the hauntings. According to legend, they refuse to mention the ghostly activity because of worries that it would stop people from visiting. More likely, it's to protect the people who still live there. Residents of the house claim that the biggest problem they experienced was with people trying to look through their windows at night.

The Hertzler House is not the only haunted site at George Rogers Clark Park; see also the Davidson Interpretive Center. Supposedly this is the exact site of the Battle of Pickuwe or Battle of Piqua. Other stories are told about the woods and area around the park, with visitors feeling uncomfortable in the area or even seeing people dressed in old-fashioned clothing. Others tell stories of seeing Native Americans and even Daniel Boone in the park.

Hospitals see a lot of death, which might explain why so many are haunted, including Mercy Hospital in Clark County. A small boy wearing jeans and a light-colored jacket is sometimes seen in the hallway. Doctors and nurses have seen the boy and had patients ask about him.

The Springfield North High School has two spirits residing in the auditorium, though neither is a former student of the school. Right across the street from the school is a series of homes, but this site was once the children's home for the county. Poor and orphaned children lived in the building, and enough died that a cemetery was built right across the street, exactly where the school auditorium stands.

Prior to the building of the school, officials dug up the graves and moved the dead children to a new location. Unfortunately, they never found a male and female who were buried there, even after looking through the records. Students claim that the ghosts of those two children still haunt the auditorium.

Gunn Road is haunted by the ghost of a boy who was hit by a car and killed there years ago. Many believe he remains because his killer drove off and was never identified. If you stop your car on the exact spot where he died and turn off the engine, legend says that it won't start.

On the outskirts of Springfield is Rockway School. A male student was in the basement one day when the boiler exploded. He either died from smoke inhalation or was burned before anyone could rescue him. Late at night, visitors catch the scent of smoke in the area and hear odd voices coming from the building.

Clark County is also home to Wittenberg University, which has several haunted spots of its own. The largest and most famous is Myers Hall. The history of the building dates back to the Civil War, when it served

Clark County

Wittenberg's Myers Hall is one of the most famous haunted sites in the county. *Courtesy of user Morhange, via Wikimedia Commons.*

as a hospital. One of the soldiers wanted to see his trusty steed before he died. The doctors agreed and brought the horse into the building, only to discover that it wouldn't leave. It's said that the man repeatedly asked for the horse and demanded it, which irritated the other patients. Doctors only allowed the horse to enter the premises to protect the health of the other patients.

One version of the story claims that the horse was actually brought inside by the soldier's friends or relatives. They placed cloth bags over the horse's hooves to keep it from disrupting some of the other patients. One man woke in the middle of the night and saw the pale white horse walking past his room. Taking it as an omen of his approaching death, he never forgot the image and experienced mental problems as a result.

Workers at the hospital tried everything they could to remove the horse, but to no avail. Eventually the horse was shot and its body moved from the building. Students and workers have occasionally heard the sounds of a horse walking through the halls. Another version claims the soldier was actually a general, but no proof has ever appeared that shows the building was a Civil War hospital.

Some say that the horse reacted badly to being taken inside, perhaps because he sensed the impending death of his owner, as some animals do. He shook, raced around the room and made a nuisance of himself, even kicking a man in the room. The men were ordered to kill the horse and shot it in the head. They then dragged its poor body down the stairs and out of the hospital.

Wittenberg's Sigma Kappa house is also haunted. Gus Sun, who owned a theater in the area and was well known among the vaudeville crowd, died in the building, as did his daughter.

A few miles away from the city limits of New Carlisle is the Blacks Cemetery. The Blacks family was buried here for years, and locals report seeing some odd things. Those passing by at night have sometimes seen a ghostly figure walking through the cemetery. Reports of odd lights and strange voices talking in the cemetery are also found.

The Plattsburg area is home to a haunted schoolhouse on Route 54. The schoolhouse sits dark and shuttered, abandoned to the elements. Some who visited the school claimed to hear and see a young girl running around. According to the rumors, she died in the school.

CHAPTER 9
GREENE COUNTY

A trip through Miami Valley's Greene County is sometimes like taking a step back in time. Between the quaint village of Clifton and the picturesque setting of Yellow Springs, it's easy to feel relaxed, as if you're stepping into another era. When you visit Greene County, you'll find a number of haunted locations. The first is Little Sugar Creek in Bellbrook. A poor young woman living in the area had the misfortune of falling in love with the mayor, though some claim it was actually a different politician from the area.

Regardless of his identity, they embarked on an ill-fated love affair that ended when she became pregnant. It's said that she took their child to see him, thinking that he would change his mind once he laid eyes on his own baby. Instead, he threw her off his property. She then threw herself into the creek, killing herself and the child.

Legend says that the girl stayed loyal to him forever. The midwife who presided over the birth did so only because she anticipated learning the father of the child. Locals whispered about the true identity. Despite going through a difficult birth, the girl bore it and refused to name the father.

Supposedly the deaths happened in June, as people report seeing the woman in June walking along the creek and singing to her child. It's sometimes said that she worked as a servant for the man and he threw her coldly into the streets when she became pregnant. Rather than confess the sordid tale of his affair to his wife, he told her that the girl got in trouble by another man and would never be seen in their home again.

An old drawing clearly shows Xenia and Wilberforce University as separate areas, while they're now closely connected. *Courtesy of the Library of Congress.*

Prairie Ghosts has a slightly darker version of the story that claims that the girl turned to a life of prostitution, as it was her only chance to support her child. Once the baby was born, it looked so much like its father that she had no choice but to keep it tightly wrapped and hidden away. She remained loyal to her former lover, not wanting anyone to know their history together.

The legend says that some saw her on the bridge, singing and talking to her baby. When she wasn't seen for a few days, locals began a search that ended when her body appeared in the water. She still held a blanket in her arms, but the baby had disappeared. No trace of the child was ever found.

Bellbrook is sometimes referred to as Ohio's Sleepy Hollow, simply because of the ghosts residing there. In addition to the young woman is James Buckley. Buckley lived along Little Sugar Creek in a small log cabin and ran his own sawmill. The sawmill quickly grew bigger, turning him into a rich man. As he lived alone and away from town, it wasn't surprising when men broke into his home and killed him.

The police arrived at the scene, finding his headless body outside the cabin. Though they searched for his head, it was never found. People who wandered around the property claimed to see a headless ghost. The ghost always held its arms out, as if asking for help. A couple who lived in the cabin even saw Buckley, carrying his head with him. The cabin and sawmill are long gone today, but the headless ghost still lingers.

Nearby Byron has the haunted Trebein Road. According to legend, a young woman was riding in a carriage on her wedding day to meet her groom. The carriage struck a rock, and she was thrown from inside. She broke her neck when she hit the ground. When word reached the wedding, her groom and father returned to the scene.

The two heartbroken men dug the large rock from the middle of the road and carried it off to the side. The rock still sits on the side of the road. Occasionally, the ghost of the young woman appears to drivers passing down the road. Sometimes she looks like a woman in white whom travelers can see through, but other times she looks like an ordinary woman. Stories vary as to when she appears: the date of her funeral, the date of her death or her birthday.

McCaslin was a farmer living in Yellow Springs, but history has long forgotten his first name. When his neighbor was shot, police confronted him. They found a piece of paper in his pocket with buckshot on it. They immediately transferred him to the police station, where they housed him in a cell once used by a man named Ramsbottom.

Ramsbottom had killed his wife in their own kitchen, slitting her throat with a knife. Sentenced to death, he stayed in that cell until the sentence was carried out. His last visitors brought him chewing tobacco, and he chewed his last bit as he took his last breath.

The police turned the accommodations into a joke for McCaslin, teasing him about sitting in the former murderer's cell. McCaslin proclaimed his innocence repeatedly and even told police that he had an alibi, but they refused to listen. The next morning when they checked the cell, they found McCaslin hanging in his cell. His suicide note simply said, "Ramsbottom, I'm coming." Some believe that during the night, he came face to face with the ghost of the dead murderer.

Xenia has several haunted locations, including the Blue Jacket Amphitheater. The theater puts on several performances ever year in an outdoor setting. Guests, workers and actors have seen the ghosts of Native Americans appearing on the stage.

A 1958 bi-level house in Xenia is the site of a bizarre haunting. A former owner swears he saw a wolf-like creature standing in the kitchen and cooking. The ghost had a violent temperament and sometimes hit people in the house, as well as banging around upstairs when the family was downstairs. It's believed that the ghost is somehow connected to the Native American burial grounds in the area.

Downtown Xenia has come a long way in recent years. *Courtesy of user Willjay, via Wikimedia Commons.*

Legend says that the Old Veterans Children Home is also haunted. The Ohio Soldiers' and Sailors' Orphans' Home was opened in Xenia in 1869 by the Grand Army of the Republic. The purpose of the children's home was to provide a safe home for children whose fathers died in the Civil War and needed a place to live. The State of Ohio took control of the building in 1870 and took in seventy-five kids.

It quickly became clear that more space was needed, especially when children were turned away. In the early part of the twentieth century, more than nine hundred children lived there. The building changed names again in 1978 when it became the Ohio Veterans' Children's Home. Its doors were finally closed in 1997, and the state sold the property to Legacy Ministries International. People report hearing sounds of kids playing and giggling.

Xenia's Eden Hall was originally built in 1840 by local man Abraham Hivling. Hivling hired free slaves to work on his farm, and those men created the bricks used to build the house. His family remained in the house until they sold it to a niece in 1881. Helen Hoover Santmeyer even included the house in her book *And Ladies of the Club…* The niece, in turn, gave the house to her daughter and son-in-law, Colonel Coates and Mary Kinney.

They entertained frequently at the home. Famous guests included John Hay and William McKinley. Their daughter, Clara Shields, remained in the home until 1972, when she passed away. Shields referred to the house as a "piece of Eden," which led to its name. The new owners, Paul Cozatt and his wife, purchased the house after her death and completed the restoration work.

Greene County

Original details surround the house at every corner. A brick arch in the basement marks the old entrance to a tunnel used as a hiding place for the Underground Railroad. A stone piece found in the house was formerly used to keep food cold before the invention of the refrigerator.

One of Kinney's daughters is believed to haunt the third floor. Supposedly the girl was hard to get along with and something of an eccentric. She and her father had problems, and she did whatever she could to spite him, including wearing off-the-wall clothing. Slamming doors and cold spots are often experienced in this area. The owners have also heard the sounds of old-fashioned music and people having fun at a party downstairs.

Eden Hall has dozens of stories told about it. Workers have found small footprints the size of children's feet marking the dust in the mornings and felt cold spots. There are also stories told about people seeing lights moving inside the building and hearing doors open and close. The sound of mysterious music also appears in the house. Locals believe at least one ghost was a woman who once lived in the building.

Spring Hill Elementary is haunted by a former teacher. Legend says that the woman was killed at the school during the late 1800s or early 1900s. She's sometimes seen wandering through the school and around the property, as if looking for the man who killed her.

Greene County is also home to Yellow Springs, which has its own haunted locations. G. Stanley Hall, which was previously used by Antioch College, is one of those haunted spots. When the school stopped using the building, it sat empty for a number of years. Numerous people have reported seeing misty figures floating through the area. The mists were even seen when the students used the building.

Antioch's Dodd Hall is also haunted. Many students believe the ghost is a young boy because of his size and the smallness of his hands. Students report having the boy jump on them in the middle of the night, as if wanting to play. As he sometimes tries to hold hands, some believe that he misses his family and wants company.

Located near Antioch College is the Glen Helen Nature Preserve. Visitors claim to see the ghosts of Native Americans wandering through the area. Locals also believe Glen Helen himself haunts the land. Yet another story places the name of the ghost as Helen Birch Bartlett. Bartlett came from a wealthy family and married an equally rich man but died in 1925 from cancer. Her husband created a display in a Chicago art gallery in her name, and her father donated the land for the nature preserve.

Greene County also has the haunted John Bryan State Park. Sometimes referred to as the Twilight Man, those who see him always describe him in the same way. He has on a blue shirt and denim overalls and wears a red handkerchief or bandana around his neck. They see him around dusk, walking from the west gate toward Meredith Road, before he disappears. There's some speculation that he was one of the men who donated the land to form the park. Some out-of-towners claim that the same man can sometimes be seen sitting in a car parked near Meredith Road.

Joseph S. Saberton built a farm in what is now the John Bryan State Park. The man was from England and had problems when it came to relating to the locals. They scoffed at him for bringing a new breed of cow to the area, the jersey, and laughed when he gave them feminine names. Yet his cows produced more milk than others in the area.

When he came down with an infection and it became clear that he wouldn't recover, he requested that his body be buried in the cow pasture. The herd was sold at auction after his death, and his body was placed in the pasture. A few years later, his brother had his body moved to Chicago.

Two men decided to rent the farm after his body was removed. One night, as they sat around on the porch, they heard a man's voice. As he shouted for his dogs and cows, the men stood in shock: they recognized Joe Saberton's voice. Though no one believed their story, both men swore that they heard the former owner return to his farm one last time.

Also in Yellow Springs is the Olde Trail Tavern. Dating back to 1827, some believe that the ghost is a woman who once lived or worked in the tavern. There was a man who was killed in the tavern. He worked as a baker, working out of a bakery in the front room. Some believe the ghost was the lover of the murdered man.

Either way, this female ghost isn't happy. Those working there claim she makes noises and sometimes knocks things from the walls. She doesn't do things all the time but occasionally makes herself present. Oddly enough, only men see her spirit, and all they notice is that she wears blue.

Greene County

During the nineteenth century and into part of the twentieth century, Yellow Springs was home to a community known as Frogtown. The two communities shared a common road, Dayton Street, but that was nearly the only thing they had in common, as many said Frogtown was a community for illegal activities.

Lou Keys was a gorgeous young woman who called Frogtown home. She had more than her fair share of suitors and was always on the lookout for the next one. She became friends with Andy Hunster, the owner of the town's ice cream store. Andy was an unusual man who was missing one leg and had bad luck with the ladies. When Lou started spending more time with him, he thought she was interested.

It broke his heart when he learned that she had taken up with another man, George Koogler. Not only did he have to live in a town where the woman he loved took up with another but he also had to see them wandering by his store, holding hands as George sang. That all came to a stop when Lou and George were found dead.

George lay on the sidewalk, murdered as he went calling on his girl. Lou lay inside, an ice pick stuck in one eye and her face smashed into pieces. The murderer used a hatchet to crush and open their skulls. Locals immediately pointed the finger of blame at Andy, but he was never found guilty of the crimes.

The case went to trial, and not long after he was acquitted, Andy burst into a friend's shop, telling him that he had seen the couple walking down the street together, just as they had in life. The man refused to believe his story, until he too heard the sound of a man singing. It was George's voice, still singing the same song he sang to Lou.

Just outside Yellow Springs is the site of a story told for years. In the early twentieth century, a young woman left her home to pick some fresh berries. She sat down, ate some of the fruit for lunch and then fell asleep. She awakened to the sounds of thunder and barely made it under a large tree before the sky opened and rain poured down. Hiding under the tree was a mistake, as lightning struck her there.

Legend says that she saw her body catch on fire just before she died. When she hadn't returned by nightfall, her husband and neighbors organized a search party. They found her still standing under the tree, her arms in the air and her mouth frozen in a scream. Rumors spread among the locals that the mortician had to sew her mouth closed and break her outstretched arms simply to make her body fit in the casket.

Not long after, people who traveled down this stretch of road after dark were occasionally greeted by a gruesome sight, especially if they were caught in a storm. The first was a salesman traveling from Springfield who saw a woman outlined in white standing under a tree and screaming. Though he couldn't hear the sounds, he knew she was screaming. He also smelled her skin burning.

He stopped at the Neff Hotel in Yellow Springs and told anyone who would listen about what he experienced. No one knew what to believe. Though he was well known in the area and locals didn't believe he would lie, they also weren't sure if he actually saw the woman. Then more people began stopping and telling locals similar stories about the woman in white.

Springfield resident Dr. William Haffner was a skeptic until he saw the woman for himself. While driving back to Springfield one night, he saw the female figure standing under the tree. He noted the way the flames licked at her body and the way her mouth hung open, though no sound came out. It's said that you might still come across the poor woman, stuck forever under the same tree. Be careful when traveling through the area during the early summer, which is the time of year when she took her last breaths.

Not far from Yellow Springs is the small village of Clifton, which has a crybaby bridge legend. The basic story remains the same, including the poor mother who killed her child and then killed herself by throwing herself off the bridge. Many people have heard what sounds like a baby screaming or crying. Others claim that the sounds are actually coming from the nearby peacock farm. Apparently, the sounds peacocks make sound almost exactly like a baby crying.

A crybaby bridge legend in Xenia offers a twist on the classic legend and updates it. The legend says that a woman was driving home one night during a storm with her child sitting next to her. The bridge ahead was washed out, but she didn't see it until it was too late. The car plunged off the bridge, hitting the creek below and killing her and the baby. They both haunt the bridge but are more frequently heard during rainstorms. In another version of the story, the mother died but the child lived for another few days. It spent its last days screaming and crying for its mother.

Greene County

The Dayton suburb of Beavercreek is home to a haunted house located near Ankeney Road. This old farmhouse dates back to the 1880s, and past residents have experienced some odd things. Former owners reported hearing the sounds of people walking around and something scratching inside the walls. Some residents have even seen a woman in white materializing from a mist.

Another haunted house in Beavercreek was built in 1957. Modern owners of the house believe the ghost is that of its original owner. He's been spotted walking around the kitchen and dining room area and also makes himself known in different ways. Those living inside the house smelled an overripe fruit smell and had lights come on suddenly and abruptly.

The small town of Alpha also has its own ghost story that is attached to a 1929 Sears home. The original owner of the house ordered the pieces from the catalogue and later assembled the Cape Cod–style house. Owners of the home felt the presence of several ghosts in the house, including a woman dressed in clothing popular during the 1930s. The main activity takes place in the kitchen, where cabinet doors open of their own accord and the smell of perfume hangs in the air. An elderly woman lived in the house in the 1940s and felt her back break when she fell down the stairs. She made it halfway across the house before she died.

Greene County is also known as the home of the Wright-Patterson Air Force Base, though portions of the base also lie in Montgomery County. The base is one of the largest in the country and is involved in top-secret missions and experiments, leading to some of the stories told about the base.

My father worked at the base for over thirty years, and I remember driving onto the base numerous times as a child, picking him up for lunch or meeting him with my mother. I also remember my brothers pointing out landmarks on the base, telling me that they housed aliens there. It's impossible to live in the area without running into someone who works there or has a family member who works there. Friends passed along stories, not only of aliens but also of overgrown cows housed in a secret building due to an experiment gone wrong.

The Wright-Patterson Air Force Base also has a few ghost stories. The stories were popular enough to entice TAPS, the group behind the popular television show *Ghost Hunters*, to Dayton for an investigation. The group investigated the most popular haunted buildings and found some evidence to prove the stories.

Area C is one of the most haunted places on the base. Building 70 is haunted by an elderly woman, but no one knows who she is or why she haunts the building. It's possible that the ghost dates back to the time before the base took over the building. Today it's used for storage and as office space. When the building wasn't in use, people passing by sometimes heard crashing sounds coming from inside. Her ghost is sometimes seen by workers, and some even claim she called out to them.

Building 219, which is also in Area C, is haunted by the ghost of a little boy. Prior to the base taking over the building, it was a hospital and pediatric clinic. Many believe the little boy died in the hospital. This ghost likes to play with the lights and doors, as well as playing with the elevators. The sounds of a young boy laughing in the basement are also reported.

Also in Area C is the haunted Arnold House. Henry E. Hebble built a basic house on the site in 1841, complete with brick walls and a brick roof. Later residents added a new roof and porches, as well as another house on the property. The house was within direct view of Huffman Prairie, the location the Wright brothers picked to practice new planes and flights. Until 1916, the home's residents watched the Wright brothers work on their planes and train pilots.

The Miami Conservancy District took over ownership of the property and, in turn, leased the property to the U.S. government following the start of World War I. In 1924, the Dayton Air Service Committee purchased a tract of land that included the house. Major Henry A. "Hap" Arnold lived in the home starting in 1929. Having trained under the Wright brothers, he frequently invited Orville Wright into the house that would eventually bear his name.

The Arnold House was used as the quarters for the commanding officer of the Fairfield Immediate Depot until 1933. Starting in 1937, it was used as an induction center and headquarters for the base squadron. By 1946, it was once again used for officers and their families. The building was officially closed in 1980 and used for storage.

The base eventually spent $100,000 to restore the building and make it a Heritage Center. It was named for General Arnold, as he was the only five-star commander in the air force. The house is now used as office space, and many people who worked in the building have reported unusual activity, especially in recent years. Those working in the building alone report hearing people talking or whispering and walk around. Stories are also told about the sounds of kids giggling in the house. Maybe the children of a former resident never moved on. Even more unusual are the stories of General Arnold himself being seen inside the building.

Wright Patterson also has ghosts roaming through other parts of the base. Full-body spirits are sometimes seen, and soldiers working late at night have heard the sound of footsteps when no one else is there. In different areas of the base, there are also stories of dark shadows wandering around. Those dark shadows may relate to the long told stories surrounding aliens at the base. While it doesn't fall under the banner of ghosts, it's an interesting story.

Conspiracy theorists claim that Wright-Patterson was the main force behind Project Blue Book. Project Blue Book began in the 1940s as a way to document and investigate any reports of unidentified flying objects (UFOs). Project Blue Book lasted until 1969 and recorded over twelve thousand UFO sightings. Over seven hundred of those cases were never solved.

Hangar 18 at the base is also home to multiple stories. Conspiracy theorists believe that Hangar 18 is home to both alien bodies and spacecraft. Legend says that after the alien crash in Roswell, New Mexico, the spacecraft and several of the bodies were sent to Wright-Patterson. A crash that occurred in Aztec, New Mexico, in 1948 was also sent back to the base.

The stories are so prevalent that it's hard to find a book or documentary on aliens that doesn't include this air force base. High-ranking government officials were denied access to certain files and buildings on base because of the aliens, or so say the stories. Whether there are actually aliens on the base, it certainly adds a little more interest to the region.

CHAPTER 10
PREBLE COUNTY

Preble County isn't the largest county in Ohio or the Miami Valley area, but it does have several haunted sites worth mentioning. This county was officially designated in 1808 when sections of Montgomery County and Butler County were set aside. Citizens named the county after a marine officer named Edward Preble, who served in the American Revolutionary War.

The first such haunted site is the Devil's Backbone in Camden. The Devil's Backbone is a gorge that overlooks Paint Creek. Native Americans who once lived in the area used the gorge as a final resting place for their leaders and chiefs.

According to legend, the men carried their leaders to the spot and left their bodies there. They were warned about touching the bones left behind, and many feared what would happen if they disobeyed. Chief Red Turtle of the Miami tribe supposedly placed a curse on the site after the white settlers forced him away. As early as the 1800s, locals claimed that the ghosts of the Indians left there were wandering the gorge because the white people moved their bones.

An alternative version of the legend claims that the leaders of the tribe were murdered by a group of white men, possibly while meditating or praying along the Devil's Backbone. The ghosts haunt the area because their bones were left on the ridge, baking in the sun. Supposedly a group of white settlers who moved to the area later were slaughtered near the gorge. Legend says that the curse of Chief Red Turtle came true.

Preble County

Camden is also home to a crybaby bridge, but the story for this one is slightly different. This story involves a young mother who became distraught after her child died. In a fit of depression, she hanged herself from the bridge. Locals claim that if you drive onto the bridge and turn your car off, you'll hear the sounds of a baby crying. An alternate version claims that you must cry for "mama" three times.

Fort St. Clair in Eaton has two separate ghosts. One is known as Gory Head and Bloody Bones. The other is a Native American. Locals claim to see the ghost dancing or moving around a fire near the graveyard in the ravine.

Eaton also has its own crybaby bridge legend. The story follows the same one as told in stories across the state. It involves a poor young woman throwing herself and her child over the side. Unfortunately, there's no record of an actual incident occurring of this nature in Eaton, and the story is told about multiple bridges in the town.

The cemetery on Lexington Road in Eaton is also rumored to be haunted. Known as the Bell Cemetery, visitors report feeling someone watching them, hearing odd noises and seeing white objects. Ghostly orbs have even appeared in photographs taken at the cemetery. Supposedly the caretakers of the cemetery installed new fences and padlocks to keep people out after experiencing a rash of vandalism.

Gratis is a small town in Preble County that's home to the haunted Brubaker Bridge. Crossing Sam's Run Creek, the bridge was built in 1887. Local legend says that in the 1930s, a group of teenagers visited Grange Hall before heading home. They went around the nearby curve too fast and crashed into the bridge. The bodies of the teens flew from the car and into the surrounding areas.

Oddly enough, no one knew the accident happened. A nearby farmer looking after his livestock saw the bodies of the teens lying on the road and on his land. Locals searched the area and thought they found the missing teens, eventually finding twelve bodies. However, one was still missing. No one at the party realized that he left with the group and was thrown under the bridge. Locals claim that his parents assumed he ran away, and eventually his body washed out and disappeared yet again.

There are many stories told about the bridge; the most common are about the missing boy. Some claim that if you stop your car on the bridge, you'll hear the sound of someone tapping on your window. It's the boy trying to get someone to notice him. Others have experienced their car dying on the bridge, hearing the tapping sound and hearing an odd hissing noise.

In her book *Spooky Ohio*, Chris Woodyard expands on the story. She claims that the farmer who found the bodies experienced his own ghostly encounter with the teens. Just a few days after the accident, he and his wife were crossing over the bridge when their car died. They heard the hissing sound and then heard thirteen taps against their car. The same thing happened multiple times to others in the area. That was how they discovered that they never found one of the missing teens.

Fudge Road in Gratis is also haunted, though no one seems to know why. Numerous people report having car problems on this stretch of road, especially at night. Their cars die suddenly and unexpectedly. It takes a few minutes before the car starts moving again. Stories are also told about floating lights alongside the road.

Fudge Road has other stories told as well, especially where the road leads into Montgomery County. One is the story of an ill-fated drug bust. Two men were killed when police burst into the house, hoping to break up a drug operation. Reports of the men's ghosts inside the house led to officials fencing off the property.

Another story involves a creature referred to as the Fudge Beast. This large, white beast has both human and animal characteristics and is sometimes seen along the side of the road. There's also a legend about a dwarf house, a tiny house that's undersized in all ways and sometimes seems to disappear.

Some believe that this stretch of road has a crybaby bridge story, as well as a spooky living woman. The story says that a young woman in town didn't have much money or many friends. She fell for the lines of a rich and smooth-talking older man who swept her off her feet. When she became pregnant, he demanded she get rid of the child. He then cut her out of his life.

After the child was born, she struggled to find help. Eventually, she took to wandering up and down Fudge Road with her baby, just hoping that someone would take pity on them, stop and give them some food. With both her and her baby starving, she decided death was a better option. She threw the child off the bridge and then jumped herself. The ghostly sounds of the baby crying can still be heard on the anniversary of his death.

Preble County

Another story is told about a woman living on Fudge Road. The stories claim that the woman owns a large number of homes on the road, all of them side by side. She lives in several of the houses, bouncing back and forth between the properties, but also rents out many of the homes. It's said that she's somehow related to the girl who killed herself and her child and is protecting the area by running off trespassers and ghost hunters.

Preble County also has the haunted Lanier School in West Alexandria. The police in this area know the school by name, mainly because of the large number of phone calls they've received about it in the past. Police are called to the school on reports of lights and things moving inside the school, as well as odd sounds. The police have never found anyone or anything inside.

Supposedly two farmhouses located near the school are also haunted. Legend says that a ditch running along State Route 503 near the houses and the school has a carved face in the rocks. Native Americans living in the area carved the face into the rocks as a way of cursing the white settlers. Locals claim that the face is frowning because the natives used the land for ceremonies but were forced out by the settlers.

Also in Preble County is the legend of a Bigfoot-style monster or creature. Unlike other creature stories in the Miami Valley, this one isn't that old, only dating back to 1977. Two boys walking near the Roberts Covered Bridge smelled a scent similar to sulfur. Turning, they spotted a creature they described as five hundred pounds and standing at least nine feet tall. They told their story to the local police, also describing the dark brown fur of the creature.

Needless to say, police didn't believe the boys' story. The police visited the spot and found unusually shaped footprints, nearly fifteen inches long. They later received reports of goat and cattle mutilations in the vicinity of the first sighting. No one ever determined what caused the footprints or what it was that the boys spotted that day. Locals began referring to the creature as the white Bigfoot because the boys claimed it had pale white eyes. There weren't any reports of the creature following that day.

WORKS CITED

Baer, Sandra. "Survey Seeks Historical Information." *Dayton Daily News*, March 5, 1998.

Clark, John R. "Reporter's Career: 50 Colorful Years." *Cincinnati Enquirer*, April 15, 1998.

Clark, Michael D. "Butler County Corpse Is Gruesome Reminder." *Cincinnati Post*, April 15, 1998.

Crout, George. *Madison Township Bicentennial Sketches (1799–1999)*. N.p.: 1998.

Forgotten Ohio. www.forgottenoh.com.

Fornshell, Marvin E. *The Historical and Illustrated Ohio Penitentiary*. N.p.: 1908.

Gerrick, David J. *Ohio's Ghostly Greats*. Dayton, OH: Dayton Press, 1982.

Ghosts of the Prairie. "Restless Ghosts." www.prairieghosts.com/ohio1.html.

The History of Clark County, Ohio. Chicago: W.H. Beers & Co., 1881.

Kraus, Fred. "College Moving Forward, Going Green." *Antiochan* (Spring 2001).

Works Cited

Leslie, Edward E. *Desperate Journeys, Abandoned Souls*. Boston: Houghton Mifflin Company, 1988.

Linn, Patricia L. *Antioch Record* 57, no. 24 (Spring 2002).

McNutt, Randy. "Peters Factory a Giant in Ruins." *Cincinnati Enquirer*, October 19, 2004.

Ohio Exploration Society. www.ohioexploration.com.

Page, Doug. "Piqua Public Library Searches for New Home." *Dayton Daily News*, January 2, 2003.

Shadowlands. "Haunted Places in Ohio." theshadowlands.net/places/ohio.htm.

Smith, Robin. *Columbus Ghosts II*. Worthington, OH: Emuses, Inc., 2003.

Willis, James A., Andrew Henderson and Loren Coleman. *Weird Ohio*. New York: Sterling Publishing Inc., 2006.

Woodyard, Chris. *Haunted Ohio*. Beavercreek, OH: Kestrel Publications, 1991.

———. *Haunted Ohio II*. Beavercreek, OH: Kestrel Publications, 1992.

———. *Haunted Ohio III*. Beavercreek, OH: Kestrel Publications, 1994.

———. *Haunted Ohio IV*. Beavercreek, OH: Kestrel Publications, 1997.

———. *Haunted Ohio V*. Dayton, OH: Kestrel Publications, 2003.

ABOUT THE AUTHOR

Jennifer Eblin is a Miami Valley native through and through. She attended the University of Dayton, finishing degrees in psychology and history. After working for a nonprofit historic preservation organization in Indiana and completing a graduate degree in historic preservation, she returned to the Miami Valley. She enjoys reading and learning more about architecture and history, watching horror movies and pretending that ghosts don't scare her. Eblin currently resides in Franklin with her boyfriend and two black cats. Find out more about her and the haunted region at the book's Facebook page, www.facebook.com/hauntedmv.

Visit us at
www.historypress.net

www.ingramcontent.com/pod-product-compliance
Lightning Source LLC
Chambersburg PA
CBHW042144160426
43201CB00022B/2406